★ **ALI** ★

AN AMERICAN CHAMPION

ALSO BY BARRY DENENBERG

Lincoln Shot: A President's Life Remembered

Titanic *Sinks!*

Nelson Mandela: No Easy Walk to Freedom—
The Complete Life Story (1918–2013)

ALI

★ AN AMERICAN CHAMPION ★

BARRY DENENBERG

Simon & Schuster Books for Young Readers
New York London Toronto Sydney New Delhi

SIMON & SCHUSTER BOOKS FOR YOUNG READERS
An imprint of Simon & Schuster Children's Publishing Division
1230 Avenue of the Americas, New York, New York 10020

For information about special discounts for bulk purchases, please contact Simon & Schuster Special Sales
at 1-866-506-1949 or business@simonandschuster.com.
The Simon & Schuster Speakers Bureau can bring authors to your live event.
For more information or to book an event, contact the Simon & Schuster Speakers Bureau
at 1-866-248-3049 or visit our website at www.simonspeakers.com.
Also available in a Simon & Schuster Books for Young Readers hardcover edition
Book design by Gordon Vanderkamp
Manufactured in China
0517 SCP
First Simon & Schuster Books for Young Readers paperback edition July 2017
2 4 6 8 10 9 7 5 3 1
The Library of Congress has cataloged the hardcover edition as follows:
Denenberg, Barry.
Ali : an American champion / Barry Denenberg.
p. cm.
ISBN 978-1-4814-0141-8 (hardcover) — ISBN 978-1-4814-0143-2 (eBook)
1. Ali, Muhammad, 1942– —Juvenile literature.
2. Boxers (Sports)—United States—Biography—Juvenile literature. I. Title.
V1132.A4D44 2014
796.83092—dc23
[B]
2013045383
ISBN 978-1-4814-0142-5 (pbk)

For Holden

Waldo Branch Library
Kansas City Public Library

Date charged: 10/28/2022,
12:58
Item ID: 0000185501087
Title: Ali : an American
champion
Date due: 11/18/2022,23:
59

Date charged: 10/28/2022,
12:58
Item ID: 0000187989850
Title: Spiders
Date due: 11/18/2022,23:
59

Thank You
816-701-3486

ACKNOWLEDGMENTS

There would be no *Ali* without the caring, intelligence, and hard work of Kristin Ostby, Greg Stadnyk, Krista Vossen, Jenica Nasworthy, Chava Wolin, Justin Chanda, and the entire Simon & Schuster Books for Young Readers team; Kathy Anderson; Lisa Smith; and, as always, Emma and Jean Feiwel.

Author's Note

The legend that is Muhammad Ali overshadows the reality of the boy he once was and the man he became. The icon has replaced the iconoclast; the saint has obscured the rebel.

The young 1960 Olympic-gold-medal winner shook up the world and pulled off perhaps the greatest upset in sports history to become the heavyweight champion of the world. Now, however, he is better known as the genial but unsteady living legend who, despite his Parkinson's disease, was able to light the Atlanta Olympic torch in 1996. Like Elvis, the Beatles, and Nelson Mandela—all also revolutionaries in their own right—Muhammad Ali's story in the popular culture has lost much of its significance; it has been sanitized and transformed into something easily digestible and unthreatening.

Back in Ali's heyday, it wasn't that way. To many, he was annoying, agitating, and defiant. Despite his boyish charm and good looks, he was a deeply unpopular figure.

Though he was largely unpopular with both white and black Americans, his exploits inside the ring (including some of the greatest fights in boxing history) and outside—boldly announcing he belonged to a highly controversial black nationalist organization and was changing his name—inspired many black Americans to be proud. He was talking about black power two years before the term came into use.

At the peak of his career, he took on the US government over a war that he (and an increasing number of other Americans) considered immoral and unjust. By example, he showed countless others that they too could stand up for their principles if they were willing, like him, to pay the price.

Muhammad Ali symbolizes and embodies those extraordinary times, but more important, he played a critical role in shaping them.

Ali: An American Champion is designed to transport the reader back in time; to provide a sense of immediacy and recreate a feeling of being present at the creation as Cassius Clay became Muhammad Ali—the catalyst of and target for heated and diverse opinions. To achieve that goal, it is composed primarily of various fictional publications and other media outlets that I have created, as well as fictional authors and interviewees. These pieces include:

- articles from local newspapers, sports and cultural magazines, and black periodicals
- "man-on-the-street" interviews
- letters to the editor
- "breaking news" radio and TV transmissions

All of these pieces have been written by me, based on meticulous and exhaustive research (see bibliography).

Carefully selected photographs, accompanied by extensive captions and a detailed history of current events, place Ali in the context of the sixties and seventies—a time when the civil rights movement blossomed and reached its apex, converging with the growing anti–Vietnam War movement.

Ali: An American Champion aims to remove the distorting curtain of time, eliminate the dubious benefits of hindsight, and reveal the true story of Muhammad Ali—the real, incredibly dynamic, and complicated person many of us have forgotten and most of us never knew.

Young Cassius

Age: Twelve
Weight: Eighty-nine pounds

In October 1954, twelve-year-old Cassius Clay left his brand-new red-and-white Schwinn outside the Columbia Auditorium in Louisville, Kentucky. Inside, he and his best friend ate their fill of free popcorn and candy.

When they left, Cassius discovered that someone had taken his bike. Furious, he told an off-duty policeman who ran a boxing gym in the basement of the building that he was going to make whoever it was pay. The policeman suggested that he might want to learn to box first.

Cassius Clay had lost his bike but found his future. He made his ring debut soon after, weighing in at eighty-nine pounds.

Louisville Sun-Times

Hometown Boy Loses Bike but Finds His Future

By Tom Stevens

For the first time in the long and proud history of "our town," a local lad has won not only the Amateur Athletic Union (AAU) light-heavyweight championship but the Golden Gloves Tournament of Champions as well!

His name?

Cassius Marcellus Clay Jr., and he's one of Louisville's outstanding young Negroes.

He was born on January 17, 1942, to Cassius Sr. and Odessa Clay. They live in a comfortable five-room house on an elm-lined street in the West End at 3302 Grand Avenue.

Cash, as Cassius Sr. likes to be called, paints signs for a living, and many of them can be seen on Louisville's buildings.

Cassius Sr. is outgoing and talkative—a little too much, according to some detractors, especially when it comes to his favorite subject: himself. Cash is a sharp dresser and quite a dancer—when he steps out onto the dance floor, everyone stops and watches.

Cassius Jr. is closest to his sweet, warmhearted mother, who, in addition to her child-rearing and housekeeping responsibilities, works as a domestic, rising at dawn every morning in order to catch the bus that takes her to the better part of town. There she does the cooking and cleaning (at four dollars a day) for a number of white families.

Unlike her talkative and sociable husband, she is on the quiet side and likes to keep to herself. A religious woman, she doesn't smoke or drink, and takes her two boys (Rudy is a year and a half younger than Cassius Jr.) to church with her every Sunday.

Cassius Jr. may have inherited his quick lip from his bombastic father, but it's clear his mom is the source of his compassion and concern for others, as well as his coffee-colored complexion (although he did not inherit her freckles).

According to Mrs. Clay, baby Cassius Jr. was so pretty everyone thought he was a girl! When Cassius Jr. was ten months old, he started talking—and he shows no signs of slowing down. Cassius, she says, grew very, very fast and refused to sit still even when taken out in his stroller. One of her favorite stories is about the day he accidentally loosened her two front teeth (or maybe just one—it changes with each telling) when he stretched and she failed to duck—most certainly his first left jab.

He loved to regale his mother (whom he calls Bird; she calls him GG) with stories of his big plans for the future: a nice, fancy house and car, a swimming pool, and lots and lots of kids.

When Cassius Jr. was a baby, relatives were always visiting the Clay house. Cassius loved the activity, and he loved being spoiled by aunts, uncles, and grandparents. As he grew older, he spent a lot of time at his aunt Coretta's house. It was the best place for his mother to leave him when she went to work. Aunt Coretta's house also contained a small restaurant and a bakery. When he was there, Cassius tried to eat everything in sight. He especially liked her famous homemade taffy. When he was old enough, Cassius returned the favor by babysitting.

Cassius's brother, Rudolph Clay, was a welcome addition to the family—especially as far as Cassius was concerned. The two brothers shared a room and did almost *everything* together, from riding their scooters and having rock fights to playing cowboys and Indians (Cassius was the cowboy) and shooting marbles. They hung out at the Chestnut Street YMCA, and during the summer they went to Camp Sky-Hi together. Cassius was a loving and protective older brother.

When Cassius was twelve, his father, after landing a well-paying job, gave his eldest son a brand new sixty-dollar bicycle. It was a bright red Schwinn with spotless whitewall tires. There were lights on the back and a spotlight up front. Cassius just couldn't wait to show it off.

One day, not long after he had received the Schwinn, Cassius Jr. and his best friend rode their bikes down to a yearly indoor fair known as the Louisville Home Show. At the end of the day, after having eaten more than their share of free popcorn and candy, they discovered that Cassius's brand-new bike had been stolen. Cassius Jr. was very angry and wanted to report the theft. Someone told him that Joe Martin, who ran the boxing gym in the basement of the building, was a policeman.

Martin wrote up a report, but when the teary-eyed boy said he was going to whip the thief, Martin suggested he learn to box first.

When visiting Martin's boxing gym for the first time, Cassius took a look around and was excited by the sights and smells of a real boxing gym. In one corner a boxer was hitting the speed bag. Over in another corner there were two boys who were not much older than Cassius jumping rope. In the ring one young boxer was shadowboxing so fast his arms were almost a blur.

Joe Martin gave Cassius an application for joining the gym. Boxing lessons were given from six to eight o'clock on Monday through Friday nights, he told him. Cassius tucked the application into his back pocket and headed home.

That weekend Cassius watched a local amateur boxing TV show called *Tomorrow's Champions*, produced by Joe Martin. On the show he saw Joe Martin working in the corner of a ring with one of the local amateur fighters. He told his mother that he was thinking about learning to box. They talked it over with his father. Both parents warned Cassius that there was no money to spare for carfare. But Mr. Clay thought learning to box might not be a bad idea.

Cassius had lost his bicycle, but he had found his future.

Joe Martin had been an amateur boxer before he became a policeman. He liked to spend as much time as possible coaching his young boxers. Cassius, a thin twelve-year-old, began training at Joe Martin's gym right away.

Soon Joe Martin decided that the skinny Cassius would be a good fighter for his Saturday TV show. Joe liked his never-give-up attitude. Cassius won his first fight, which was shown on *Tomorrow's Champions* on a split decision.

After his first victory Cassius started training even harder.

Somehow he managed his busy schedule. After school he went to his job at Nazareth College. There he dusted, swept the stairs, and cleaned the floors. He earned enough money to pay for his carfare to the gym. His next stop was Joe Martin's, where he trained from six to eight o'clock. Then he was off to a second gym run by a quiet Negro trainer named Fred Stone. There he trained from eight until midnight.

Cassius trained hard. He usually started with one hundred left jabs. Then he jabbed and moved forward, and jabbed and moved back. Next he did combinations—jab and hook, jab and hook—over and over. He practiced blocking punches and ducking them. His training usually ended with one hundred push-ups and one hundred deep knee bends.

As the days zipped by, he learned more. He learned how to keep moving; how to move backward at just the right time; and how to avoid punches, leaning away from them at the last second. Cassius practiced so much that

soon he could tell when a punch was coming almost *before* it was thrown. He would keep his head in range, hoping his opponent would try to hit him. Then, at just the right moment, he would lean back, just a fraction of an inch out of the way. He would step to the right or step to the left and throw a lightning-fast jab. Then he would begin moving all over again.

Each day Cassius woke up at dawn to run. He skipped rope, making it fancier and harder all the time. The more he skipped rope, the better his footwork became. He shadowboxed every day too. That helped his hand speed and his mental quickness.

Cassius started to specialize in defense. He began to develop his own way of retreating. He concentrated on the timing of his punches and when to pull back. He practiced every move until he had it memorized and he didn't have to think. If he had to think while he was fighting, he knew the punch would take too long.

As often as he could, Cassius watched fights on TV, studying each boxer's moves. And as he watched, he thought that he could beat them. Cassius didn't keep his opinion to himself. The other boys at Joe Martin's gym grew tired of Cassius's boasting and began to dislike him. It became so bad that Joe had to threaten to ban him from the gym.

In 1959 Cassius won the Louisville Golden Gloves light-heavyweight crown. He went on to fight in the Tournament of Champions in Chicago. The tournament was in a huge stadium. It was the biggest stadium Cassius had ever seen.

Louisville Sun-Times

-------------------- August 15, 1960 --------------------

An Exclusive Interview with Central High School Principal Atwood Wilson

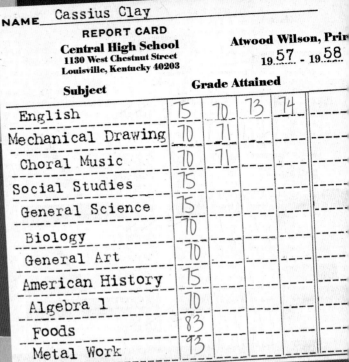

NAME	Cassius Clay						

REPORT CARD
Central High School
1130 West Chestnut Street
Louisville, Kentucky 40203

Atwood Wilson, Prin

19 57 - 19 58

Subject	Grade Attained						
English	75	70	73	74			
Mechanical Drawing	70	71					
Choral Music	70	71					
Social Studies	75						
General Science	75						
Biology	70						
General Art	70						
American History	75						
Algebra 1	70						
Foods	83						
Metal Work	93						

Atwood Wilson, sixty-five, is himself a graduate of Central High and studied at Fisk University and the University of Chicago. He became principal in 1934, and in 1948 he helped desegregate the Louisville Free Public Library.

Last month eighteen-year-old Cassius Clay graduated from Central. The six-foot, 180-pound young man has won Golden Gloves and AAU tournaments and compiled an impressive amateur light-heavyweight boxing record: 108 wins, 8 losses.

We spoke with Wilson recently about his illustrious graduate:

LOUISVILLE SUN-TIMES: Let's talk about Cassius the student before we talk about the athlete. We understand he graduated near the bottom of his class: 376th out of 391 students. Some of his teachers tell us that although he was always well behaved, he drew and daydreamed during class, and he would sometimes pretend to be announcing his name over the loudspeaker system.

ATWOOD WILSON: Cassius had difficulties with his studies; his attention span could have used improvement, there's no question about it. He is, I believe, an admirable student outside the academic world.

LST: How so?

AW: He brings so much focus and dedication to his training. Boys his age have serious trouble concentrating, so I use him as an example. Not so much because of his athletic ability—although he is an extraordinary athlete—but more to show my students that if you want to accomplish *anything* in life, you have to work hard and be committed. There's no substitute for that.

And let me mention here that many great athletes have been blessed with superior physical gifts. But the majority of them do not nurture and care for those gifts properly.

Cassius invariably follows a Spartan regimen so as not to squander his God-given talent.

Central High, as you know, is a Negro school, and we Negroes, as we enter the 1960s, must begin to question our proper place in society and how we, too, can achieve our rightful share of the American dream.

LST: Former classmates we've spoken to say Cassius made no bones about the fact that he is destined for greatness.

AW: Oh, yes, he was not shy about that.

LST: Is it true that you actually introduced the young man during assemblies by saying: "Here he is, ladies and gentlemen! Cassius Clay! The next heavyweight champion of the world"?

AW: Yes, and I believed every word of it.

He was never mean and never resorted to physical violence—with one exception.

LST: Can you tell us about it?

AW: Once—and I'm not sure what precipitated the incident—a boy called him a name and swung a T square at Cassius, who understandably took exception to this. Cassius knocked him out with a right to the jaw.

LST: Sounds like an open-and-shut case of self-defense.

AW: Yes, but more importantly, it was the only time he ever hit anyone.

In fact, I think boxing helped keep him *out* of trouble and ensures that he continues to head down the right road in life. Cassius always focuses on what he has to do and knows he's going places and doesn't allow anything to deter him from his goals.

Not only that, his buoyant approach to life is an invaluable lesson to his peers. You always knew which table in the cafeteria Cassius was at because that's where all the laughter was coming from.

LST: Can you confirm rumors that on graduation day, unlike the other boys, who wore dress shirts and ties under their robes, Cassius wore a T-shirt?

AW: I wouldn't know about that.

LST: Some of his female classmates told us he did lack confidence in one area: girls. In fact, they say he actually fainted the first time he kissed someone.

AW: Again, I wouldn't know about such things. I'm sure the girls are quite well informed, however.

I will say this: Despite his bragging and outgoing manner, in many ways Cassius was always a gentle and shy boy—so I'm not surprised.

LST: We're told that when students became unruly, you were known to get on the intercom and threaten, "Any acting up and I'm going to get Cassius Clay on you."

AW: Guilty as charged. And by the way, it worked.

LST: Can you tell us about your "Claim to Fame" speech, which you gave your teaching staff?

AW: You seem to have all the details right there in your little notebook. Why don't you just read it to me and I'll confirm or deny.

LST: One line in your speech said, "One day our greatest claim to fame is going to be that we knew Cassius Clay or taught him."

AW: True enough.

LST: Thank you for taking the time to talk with us, Principal Wilson.

STATEMENT OF WAGES AND DEDUCTIONS

FORM 4245

65698

Nazareth College Library
851 South Fourth Street
Nazareth, KY

Cassius Clay NAME OF EMPLOYEE

Job(s): Mowing lawns, sweeping and mopping floors, dusting books and shelves (second floor library), waxing and buffing tables, transporting books

TOTAL WAGES	DEPT.	BUREAU	PAYMENT OTHER THAN WAGES	AMOUNT PAID
Hours Worked: 10 @ $0.60 per hour				= $6.00

PAY PERIOD ENDED

MONTH	DAY	YEAR
03	20	59

_____ (signature)

Supervisor: Sister James Ellen

DETACH AND RETAIN THIS STUB

Emmett Till

In the summer of 1955 Emmett Till, a Chicago eighth grader, was brutally murdered while visiting his cousins in Mississippi. The boy's funeral and the trial (the defendants were acquitted) became a sensational national news story.

Cassius Clay was thirteen—just about the same age as Emmett—when his father showed him a magazine containing photographs of the funeral.

Rosa Parks

On Thursday, December 1, 1955, Rosa Parks boarded the bus for home after a long day of work in a downtown department store. An active member of the local NAACP (National Association for the Advancement of Colored People), Parks refused to give up her seat so that a white passenger could sit. Her courageous act precipitated the successful 382-day Montgomery, Alabama, bus boycott led by Dr. Martin Luther King.

The Supreme Court ruling banning segregation on the city's public transportation took effect on December 20, 1956. Cassius Clay was fourteen at the time.

Parks was not invited to any of the photo ops featuring Dr. King. Here she is shown (sitting front left, looking out the window) in one staged the next day by a national magazine. Ironically, the driver of the bus was the very same one who had had her arrested over a year earlier.

Sit-Ins

On February 13, 1960—seven months before Cassius Clay departed for the Rome Olympics—124 students at Nashville's Fisk University set off on their own quest.

Led by fellow students Diane Nash and John Lewis, they sat down at one of the city's whites-only lunch counters. Eventually they were attacked by local white youths, arrested by the city's police, and sent to jail.

Their bold but disciplined behavior and subsequent unfair treatment resulted in national media attention as the sit-ins spread to sixty-nine other American cities.

Here, six weeks later, a lone Negro student is seen sitting at a whites-only lunch counter.

The packages of napkins on the adjacent stools are intended to discourage others from joining him.

Cassius Clay:
Daily Workout Schedule

*Morning: Race school bus all the way to school; pass bus when it stops for students to get on

*Jump rope in halls between classes

*Shadowbox in boys' room using mirror

*Nights: 6:00-8:00: Train at Joe Martin's gym

8:00-12:00: Train at Fred Stoner's gym

jabs

hooks

blocking

ducking

moving

push-ups

deep knee bends

*No burgers, fries, sodas, or junk

*Milk with raw egg, or water with garlic

*Be dedicated

*Concentrate

*Pay the price

SPORTSWORLD WEEKLY

SEPTEMBER 5, 1960

CLAY WINS GOLD!

ELECTED UNOFFICIAL MAYOR OF OLYMPIC VILLAGE—WILL TURN PRO

By Keith Kincaid

ROME, ITALY

There were bigger names: team captain and decathlon champion Rafer Johnson; gold medal winner in the long jump, Ralph Boston; Wilma Rudolph, the track athlete who overcame polio to win three gold medals; and basketball luminaries Oscar Robertson and the two Jerrys, West and Lucas.

But the athlete everyone seems to be talking about at this, the XVII Olympiad, is the winner in the light-heavyweight boxing division: Cassius Clay of Louisville, Kentucky.

And he almost didn't make the trip.

Apparently, the fearsome and seemingly fearless pugilist is terrified of one thing.

"He was afraid of flying," his manager, Joe Martin, told Sportsworld Weekly. "We had a rough flight going to California for the trials, and so when it came to go to Rome he said he wasn't gonna fly, and that he wouldn't go. I said: 'Well, you'll lose the opportunity of being a great fighter,' and he said: 'Well, I'm not gonna go.' He wanted to take a boat or something."

The young man even went so far as to buy a parachute and keep it close by during the long flight.

His roommate, Wilbert "Skeeter" McClure, tells us this about the flash fighter: "In Rome, he was outgoing but he was seriously into boxing. I don't know of anybody . . . who took it more seriously than he did. We'd walk around and he'd go up to people and shake hands with them, but he had his mind on training. He worked for that gold medal. He trained very, very hard. . . . He was one of the hardest trainers I'd ever seen."

Clay may have been unpopular with his opponents inside the ring, but along Via Veneto and around the Olympic village it was a different story, as Wilma Rudolph reveals: "Everybody wanted to see him. Everybody wanted to be near him. Everybody wanted to talk to him."

Clay, proud as a peacock, struts around the Olympic village displaying his gold medal around his neck. Apparently, he wears it twenty-four hours a day—even sleeping and eating with it on. The poised eighteen-year-old introduces himself to his fellow Olympians (even if they don't speak his language), swaps team lapel pins, and uses up roll after roll of film taking pictures with his Brownie Hawkeye camera.

He is, by popular acclaim, "the mayor of the Olympic Village."

Ironically, the only thing the fleet-footed fighter can't do is dance.

Clay will tell anyone who cares to listen about the future he has planned for himself. A future that includes heavyweight champion of the world Floyd Patterson, whom Clay posed with and told: "Be seeing you in about two more years."

"That was my last amateur fight," Clay said as he kissed his medal. "I'm turning pro."

And perhaps there's even a career in politics for the outspoken and verbally gifted young man. When an obviously ill-intentioned Russian reporter asked him, just after the awards ceremony, about racial discrimination in America, Clay shot back: "Tell your readers we've got qualified people working on that problem, and I'm not worried about the outcome. To me, the U.S.A. is still the best country in the world, counting yours."

Spoken like a true champion.

Clay Wins Gold!

September 6, 1960. Olympic light-heavyweight boxing gold medal winner Cassius Clay is pictured with two other U.S. boxers who brought home the gold.

Louisville Sun-Times

-------------------- September 15, 1960 --------------------

A Hero's Welcome for Local Boy!

Olympic Gold Medal Winner Cassius Clay Returns Home

By Tom Stevens

His mom heard the news of her son's victory on the radio. Mrs. Odessa Clay was sitting on her back porch, but not for long. She left immediately to spread the word throughout the neighborhood.

Then she settled down to prepare a nice, big welcome-home turkey dinner— with all the trimmings—for her son. The boy's proud father painted their front steps red, white, and blue.

Mrs. Clay said she was glad her son was turning pro, because she supports him doing anything he loves, and she knows how much he loves boxing.

Looking to bask in the glory, an enthusiastic crowd of over two hundred, including friends, family, cheerleaders, a marching band, and, of course, politicians, greeted the gold medal winner at the airport and lined the streets while Cassius, accompanied by Mr. and Mrs. Clay and brother Rudy, waved from a Cadillac convertible that led a fifty-car motorcade headed for Central High School.

At a reception in city hall the mayor proclaimed: "If all young people could handle themselves as well as Clay does, we wouldn't have juvenile problems."

The Children's Crusade

Martin Luther King Jr. considered Birmingham, Alabama, the nation's most segregated city. He was jailed for leading marches aimed at forcing the white business leaders to desegregate the downtown lunch counters and public facilities and to hire black workers.

Inspired by James Bevel, who argued that students had a stake in their future, the city's black children were organized and began to march. They were arrested and jailed in huge numbers.

On the second day of what would come to be called the Children's Crusade—Friday, May 3, 1963 (a month before Cassius Clay went to London for his nineteenth professional bout)—police dogs and fire hoses were used to control the demonstrators.

This photo shows high school honor student Walter Gadsden, who was, in fact, not a demonstrator but a spectator. It appeared the next day on the front page of the *New York Times* with this headline: DOGS AND HOSES REPULSE NEGROES AT BIRMINGHAM.

Many Americans—white as well as black—were, themselves, repulsed.

Other shocking photographs showing students being sent sprawling by high-powered fire hoses also appeared on the front pages of the nation's newspapers, giving the young civil rights movement much-needed national exposure.

The March on Washington

On August 28, 1963, over 250,000 people joined the March on Washington for Jobs and Freedom (shown here in an aerial view taken from a helicopter).

It was the largest demonstration in the nation's history and involved a coordinated effort by several civil rights organizations. The unexpectedly huge turnout was considered a testament to the growing strength of the civil rights movement. The throng marched peacefully from the Washington Monument to the Lincoln Memorial, where Marian Anderson; Joan Baez; Bob Dylan; Peter, Paul, and Mary; and Mahalia Jackson (among others) sang.

The two main speakers were John Lewis (the youngest speaker) and Martin Luther King Jr., whose "I Have a Dream" speech clearly resonated with the crowd.

Nation of Islam minister Malcolm X referred to it as "the Farce on Washington" in numerous speeches. Cassius Clay first heard Malcolm speak in New York City when he returned from the Rome Olympics. Two years later, in 1962, Clay introduced himself to Malcolm, and the two became like brothers. Neither one attended the successful event.

"The Love That Forgives"

On Sunday morning, September 15, 1963—just weeks after the March on Washington—a bomb exploded in the basement of the three-story Sixteenth Street Baptist Church in Birmingham, Alabama. The church had been, in recent months, the center for civil rights activities in the city, most notably the Children's Crusade.

Four young black girls were killed in what was believed to be a racially motivated terrorist attack:

Addie Mae Collins (age fourteen)

Cynthia Wesley (age fourteen)

Carole Robertson (age fourteen)

Denise McNair (age eleven)

All four were in the church's basement preparing to return for the sermon, "The Love That Forgives."

Dallas

On November 22, 1963, John F. Kennedy, his eye on the upcoming presidential election, flew to Dallas, Texas, hoping to shore up his support in that key state. He and the First Lady were in the backseat of a Lincoln convertible—the rain had stopped, so there was no need to put up the bubble top.

Their motorcade was traveling at 11.2 mph past the cheering crowds that lined the route, which had been planned to provide maximum exposure. At 12:30 p.m. (CST) twenty-four-year-old ex-marine Lee Harvey Oswald, who was perched in a sixth-floor window of the Texas School Book Depository (where he worked), fired three shots from a high-powered rifle equipped with a telescopic lens.

This photograph—taken at precisely that moment—shows the president slumping in the backseat and his wife leaning over him. A Secret Service agent, who ran after the already accelerating vehicle as soon as he heard the first shot, managed to climb onto the

THE CONTENDER

By Keith Kincaid

It's been almost three years since we've written about Cassius Clay ("Clay Wins Gold!", September 5, 1960). Back then he was a freshly minted Olympic gold medal winner. Now he's a contender who wants a shot at the boxing championship title.

A lot has happened in those three years.

Cassius had his first professional bout on October 29, 1960, in Louisville's Freedom Hall. Over six thousand fans turned out to see their Olympic hero. All his years of hard work and training paid off. He won in a unanimous decision.

But Cassius still had a lot to learn. He would need expert training if he was to be properly prepared for the work of professional boxing. Cassius's backers, the Louisville Sponsoring Group, decided to send him to Archie Moore's training camp. Archie was one of the most experienced fighters in the business.

When Cassius set off for San Diego, his Louisville backers were sure that they had made the right decision. They were wrong. Right from the start Cassius didn't like Archie—and he didn't like the training camp either. After just a few weeks Cassius left the camp and returned home.

The Louisville Sponsoring Group then contacted a Miami-based boxing trainer named Angelo Dundee, whom Cassius had met three years earlier, in 1957, when Angelo was in Louisville with one of his fighters.

Cassius's relationship with Angelo was the most important step in his blossoming professional career. He and Angelo were a perfect match right from the beginning. Angelo was a good listener, and Cassius was a good talker. Not only that, Angelo was a family man with six kids of his own. He understood the young Cassius. He realized that he couldn't change his unique style of fighting. And he didn't try.

Cassius broke almost every boxing rule. He did not punch to the body, and he held his hands at his sides, too low to protect his face. Odd as it might have looked to the experts, this style worked for Cassius. Angelo appreciated Cassius's eccentricities and didn't tell him what to do; instead he offered "suggestions." Angelo improved Cassius's technique. Soon he was shooting his left jab with more authority, slipping away from punches more easily, and learning to punch with power. Joining Angelo was his "fight doctor," Ferdie Pacheco, who also ran clinics for many of Miami's poor minorities.

Angelo was impressed with Cassius's work ethic: "Training him was a whole different ballgame from most fighters. You didn't have to push him. It was like jet propulsion. Just touch him and he took off."

Cassius already had his mind set on beating Floyd Patterson's record. At twenty-one years and ten months old, Floyd was the youngest man ever to win the heavyweight championship. Eighteen-year-old Cassius had only three years to reach his goal.

In 1961 Cassius fought eight times and won every fight—six of them by knockouts.

He arrived on the scene at a time when the world of prime-time prizefighting had become boring and lackluster. Gone were the popular heavyweight champions of yesteryear: Jack Dempsey, Joe Louis, and Rocky Marciano. Although Louis and Marciano weren't big talkers, they had a way about them, inside and outside the ring, that inspired tens of thousands of fans—fans that Cassius Clay was starting to attract. The boy was anything but boring, and silence was something he had only heard about. He was so bold he began predicting not only the outcome of his upcoming bouts, but the round in which his opponent would fall.

Some called him the Louisville Lip and considered him nothing more than a bag of wind. But to others he was a sorely needed breath of fresh air.

In October 1961 he was about to fight Alex Miteff. Before the fight he told everyone which combination of punches would knock Miteff out. And in the sixth round Cassius knocked Miteff out with the very combination of punches that he had predicted!

Experts now rated Cassius the number eleven contender for the heavyweight title. Fight fans spoke about how brash he was. And people who had never given boxing a thought seemed to know his name.

Cassius grew bolder with every bout. Before his fight with Willi Besmanoff he told reporters, "I'm embarrassed to get into the ring with this unrated duck. I'm ready for top contenders like Patterson and Sonny Liston." He knocked out the "duck" in the seventh round.

Before his bout with Sonny Banks he promised Banks would be on the floor in four. But Banks shocked Cassius, sending *him* to the floor for the first time in his professional career. At the count of two, though, Cassius was already up.

Archie Moore, the former light-heavyweight champion, was now fighting as a heavyweight and had a match scheduled with Clay. By 1962 Archie Moore had been fighting for twenty-seven years. In his prime he had been one of the greatest fighters. Now he was flabby and out of shape. Some experts said he should not be fighting at all.

Weeks before the fight both fighters came out with their lips flapping. Cassius predicted he would beat "Moore in four." His footwork and the speed of his combinations would be too much for Archie, Cassius announced. He even had a new punch just for this fight. Cassius called it the "pension punch" and said it would retire Archie and put him on a pension.

On November 15, 1962, the talking was over and the fighting began. Seats in the Los Angeles Sports Arena were sold out, setting an indoor attendance record for California. The bout was shown on closed-circuit TV in theaters around the country.

Cassius was too much for the aging Archie. He knocked Archie down three times in the fourth round, and the fight was over.

Cassius was now twenty years old and considered by most experts to be the fourth-ranked contender for the heavyweight crown.

Cassius's next important fight was at New York City's Madison Square Garden in March 1963 against Doug Jones, a tough, smart veteran of the ring who had never been knocked out and was ranked third.

There was a New York City newspaper strike leading up to the match, and this simply would not do for attention-hungry Cassius, who wanted as much press coverage of the fight as possible. Cassius pulled out all the publicity stops. Not only did he do radio and TV shows and make the restaurant and nightclub circuit, but he stopped by bowling alleys, hung out and harangued people at street corners, and even showed up on the bill with folksingers at the Bitter End, a Greenwich Village coffeehouse. There, gracing Poetry Night with his presence, the poet of pugilism predicted:

"This boy likes to mix
so he must fall in six."

Which he revised not long after to:

"I'm changing the pick I made before
Instead of six, Doug goes in four."

Thing was, it worked; for the first time in six years the Garden was sold out.

But Jones didn't fall in four—or five, six, seven, eight, nine, or ten. He gave Cassius more trouble than he'd expected. The fight was close, but Cassius finally won, and the fans, disappointed that the Louisville Lip's predictions hadn't come to pass, started booing and throwing things—beer cans (empty), cigar stubs (unlit), and peanuts.

After the fight, Cassius, in an uncharacteristic burst of actual truth, warned, "If the fans think I can do everything I say I can do, then they're crazier than I am."

Crazy or not, the twenty-one-year-old now claims he's ready to face the heavyweight champ himself, Charles "Sonny" Liston.

WE ASKED SOME OF OUR TOWN'S MOST KNOWLEDGEABLE BOXING FANS:

WHOM DO YOU LIKE: REIGNING HEAVYWEIGHT CHAMPION CHARLES "SONNY" LISTON OR TOP-RANKED CONTENDER CASSIUS "THE LIP" CLAY?

SONNY LISTON LEARNED TO BOX WHILE HE WAS IN PRISON FOR ARMED ROBBERY. THE CON WHO TAUGHT HIM WAS SENT UP FOR GRAND THEFT AUTO. THEN THE PRISON CHAPLAIN SAW HIS POTENTIAL AND SORT OF TOOK HIM UNDER HIS WING.

LISTON'S BIG, MEAN, AND POWERFUL. HE HAS A LEFT THAT CAN TAKE A MAN OUT WITH JUST ONE PUNCH. HIS FISTS ARE SO BIG HE HAS TO HAVE HIS GLOVES MADE SPECIAL. WAIT TILL THOSE FISTS COLLIDE WITH THAT PRETTY FACE THAT LOUDMOUTH KEEPS TELLING US ABOUT.

LISTON, TKO, THIRD ROUND. BET ON IT. I DID.

LET'S START WITH THIS: LISTON'S THE GREATEST HEAVYWEIGHT SINCE JOE LOUIS, MAYBE EVEN THE GREATEST OF ALL TIME!

HE'S WON THIRTY-FIVE OF HIS LAST THIRTY-SIX FIGHTS—TWENTY-FIVE KNOCKOUTS, BY THE WAY—AND THE ONE HE LOST WAS A DECISION, NOT A KO, EVEN THOUGH THE GUY HE FOUGHT WAS LUCKY ENOUGH TO BREAK SONNY'S JAW (HE SAID THE GUY CAUGHT HIM WHEN HE WAS LAUGHING).

SPEAKING OF KOS, HE KNOCKED PATTERSON OUT IN THE FIRST ROUND. NOT ONE REIGNING HEAVYWEIGHT CHAMPION HAD EVER BEEN KO'D IN THE FIRST ROUND! LISTON NEEDED ONLY FOUR SECONDS MORE IN THE SECOND FIGHT: TWO MINUTES, TEN SECONDS.

THAT'S ABOUT HOW LONG I GIVE CLAY.

LISTON'S AN OLD MAN—DON'T YOU BELIEVE ANY OF THAT NONSENSE ABOUT HIM BEING THIRTY ANYTHING. HE'S FORTY-FIVE IF HE'S A DAY. NOT ONLY THAT, HE'S TOO FLAT FOOTED AND TOO SLOW FOR SOMEONE LIKE CASSIUS CLAY.

MARK MY WORDS: LISTON WILL BE PLODDING ALONG, TRYING TO CUT OFF THE RING, WHICH IS HIS STYLE, IF YOU WANT TO CALL IT THAT, AND TRYING TO GET CASSIUS TO HOLD STILL LONG ENOUGH FOR HIM TO LAND ONE OF THOSE LOOOONG, SLOOOW LEFTS. AIN'T GONNA WORK, PAL.

BECAUSE CLAY'S GONNA BE BOBBIN' AND WEAVIN', DUCKIN' AND DIVIN', MOVIN' IN AND OUT, DANCIN' UP ON HIS TOES AND LEANIN' BACK JUST AN INCH OUT OF REACH, HOLDIN' HIS HANDS LOW LIKE HE'S DARING LISTON TO HIT HIM, AND DRIVING THE OLD MAN CRAZY. JUST WATCH.

AND HE'LL BE WATCHIN', CLAY WILL; HE'LL BE WATCHIN' SONNY'S TIRED OLD EYES, EYES THAT SAY, *I'VE BEEN DOING THIS TOO LONG,* WATCHIN', WAITIN', ANTICIPATIN', AND THEN COUNTERING WITH STINGING JAB AFTER STINGING JAB. SONNY LISTON WILL DIE THE DEATH OF A THOUSAND CUTS.

CLAY, TKO, EIGHTH ROUND. ON CUTS.

GET THERE EARLY. LISTON, KO, ROUND ONE.

CLAY WILL PROBABLY BE ABLE TO RUN AWAY FOR THREE, MAYBE FOUR, ROUNDS BEFORE SONNY BEGINS TO ZERO IN AND LAND SOME OF THOSE HAMMERLIKE PUNCHES.

LISTON, KO, ROUND FIVE.

THIS FIGHT'S GOING TO BE A JOKE.

IT'S A MISMATCH. A CRIME. MAN AGAINST BOY. YOU TELL ME. FRANKLY, I THINK THEY'D BETTER FIGURE OUT THE FASTEST ROUTE TO THE HOSPITAL, BECAUSE THE QUESTION ISN'T WHO'S GOING TO WIN, THE QUESTION IS WILL CLAY LIVE?

I DON'T CARE IF THIS KID IS YOUNGER, FITTER, FASTER. NONE OF THAT CRAP MATTERS IF YOU GET HIT HARD ENOUGH OFTEN ENOUGH.

LISTON, KO, ROUND THREE.

A POEM À LA CASSIUS CLAY
IF CLAY IS LATE
CHALK IT UP TO FATE
'CAUSE THE "MOUTH THAT ROARED"
IS GONNA GET GORED
AND HE'D BETTER STOP, LOOK, AND LISTEN
HERE COMES A LESSON FROM LISTON
AND HE'S GONNA HAVE TROUBLE LIFTIN'
HIMSELF FROM THE FLOOR
WHEN HE'S DONE IN FOUR.

Denver, Colorado / Reported by Al Pike

It's a little after three a.m., Denver time, and top-ranked contender Cassius Clay—a.k.a. Mighty Mouth—has had the audacity (something he has in spades) to show up outside current heavyweight champion Sonny Liston's home in this wealthy suburb.

Since he turned pro three years ago, Clay has not stopped spouting bad poetry, poking fun unmercifully at his opponents, and predicting—accurately in most cases—the round they would fall. Undoubtedly, all these gyrations are designed to hype the fight, get some ink and airtime, and fill arena seats and his pockets. Some believe there's more to it. That he's so scared, he has to work himself into a frenzy to overcome that fear. Others believe that there's more method to his madness than meets the eye. His act is meant to unnerve his adversary—get him off his game. Still others believe the guy is just plain nuts. The jury, we have to report, is still out.

One thing's for certain, though: The challenger now has the world heavyweight champion squarely in his slightly skewed sights. He follows Sonny Liston everywhere, it seems.

Clay and his entourage—brother Rudy and photographer/friend Howard Bingham—drove Clay's red-and-white, thirty-passenger bus nonstop from Chicago. Apparently the fearless fighter has a fear of flying. As soon as they entered the Denver city limits, Clay called all the local radio and TV stations and the newspaper wire services to ensure what is becoming his customary coast-to-coast coverage (Clay is proving to be not only a first-rate pugilist but a master publicist). They pulled up to the curb outside Liston's home just minutes ago and directed a spotlight on the house.

Clay sent Bingham to ring the champ's doorbell, while he paced back and forth on the lawn screaming. A sleepy, not-too-happy, and very un-Sonny Liston answered the bell in his bathrobe. His demeanor is understandable considering the hour and what greeted him. Clay continued his madman act, screaming something about Liston being a "big, ugly bear" and daring him to step out onto the lawn and have a go right then and there.

For a moment it looked as if the champ just might take the kid up on it, but cooler heads, belonging to irate neighbors who called the police, prevailed.

Thus ends another chapter in the saga of the lad from Louisville—a boy who clearly dances to the beat of a different drummer.

THE FAB FOUR
(PLUS ONE)

The Beatles were in town to do *The Ed Sullivan Show* and stopped by Miami's Fifth Street Gym on February 18, 1964, for a photo op with the Louisville Lip.

Clay was late, which didn't thrill John Lennon.

"You're not as stupid as you look," the Lip quipped.

"No," replied Lennon, no slouch when it came to verbal fisticuffs, "but you are."

February 25, 1964

10:30 a.m.

LISTON vs. CLAY: Prefight Weigh-In

Reported by Nick Paglia

WLTN-TV
Miami, Florida

Clay and his entourage are here. He's wearing a denim jacket with BEAR HUNTIN' embroidered in red on the back. The "bear" being Sonny Liston, who is, as usual, ignoring it all.

Clay is running around banging a big stick on the floor and chanting, "Float like a butterfly, sting like a bee; rumble, young man, rumble," over and over again.

It's hard to tell if he's crazy, scared, or both.

There are four hundred newspaper, radio, and TV reporters from seventeen countries.

Virtually every one of the reporters believes the only question is in what round Liston, who is a 7–I favorite, will knock out the brash youngster and how badly he will be hurt. There are rumors that a route to the hospital has already been mapped out. The scene absolutely defies description.

Every one of the reporters also appears to be shocked by Clay's hysterical antics.

Now he's yelling, "I'm the champ! I'm ready to rumble!"

I have never seen anything like this in my seventeen years covering heavyweight boxing matches. Never.

Clay is clearly stark raving mad.

Now it looks like he's winking at his pal, boxing great Sugar Ray Robinson—like this is just an act he's putting on.

Liston, as per style, just stares balefully into the middle distance, paying no attention to the frenzied upstart. Wait, now he's holding up two fingers—meaning he will knock out the youngster in the second round.

The champ looks like he can't wait to get in the ring.

Clay Wins!

Liston Hit by Series of Lefts in Sixth

Spits Out Mouthpiece, Refuses to Come Out for Seventh

"Greatest upset in the history of boxing."
—Joe Louis

Cassius Clay enters the arena wearing a short white robe with THE LIP embroidered in red on the back.

Impressive first round for Clay. Turns to swells in $250 seats and yawns while still sitting on stool.

Taunts champion while jabbing effectively in third. "You big sucker; I got you now."

Clay can't see after round four. Apparently, there is something in his eyes: a burning substance of some sort. Could be liniment Liston's cornermen rubbed on his shoulder. Or Liston's corner may have "juiced" his gloves. It is not clear if this is an accident or if something is amiss. Clay's blinking frantically and yelling: "I can't see! I can't see! Cut 'em off! I can't see! Cut off the gloves."

Working methodically in the corner, savvy trainer Angelo Dundee sponges his fighter's eyes and shouts: "This is the big one, daddy! . . . We're not quitting now." He pushes Clay toward the center of the ring for the start of round five. The youngster is forced to fight

The North Star: Pointing the Way
THE NATION OF ISLAM'S NEWEST CONVERT

February 28, 1964

The morning after he stunned the sports world by winning the heavyweight championship, Cassius Clay stunned the world at large when he announced his membership in the Nation of Islam (NOI).

Elijah Muhammad, NOI's sixty-six-year-old spiritual leader, preaches that whites are a race of "blue-eyed devils." The sect is not interested in integration, and members are not allowed to march, protest, picket, demonstrate, sit in, or even register to vote. (It should be noted that the NOI philosophy is not necessarily synonymous with the Islamic religion as practiced worldwide.)

In 1952 the NOI was thought to have approximately eight hundred members and was considered an obscure organization. They became significantly more visible in 1959 when a five-part documentary, *The Hate That Hate Produced*, aired on television from July 13 to 17. Some estimate that nationwide membership in the NOI is as much as fifty thousand to seventy-five thousand.

Economic independence is a stated goal, and the men are taught practical work skills so they can get better jobs and improve themselves.

Members are required to donate 10 percent of their earnings to the organization and are required to maintain high moral standards. There is no drinking, narcotics use, smoking, gambling, dancing, moviegoing, stealing, adultery, or domestic quarrels. There are also strict dietary requirements.

The men do not straighten their hair, but keep it closely cropped. They dress neatly, in dark suits with white shirts,

"I AM THE KING!"

A jubilant Cassius Clay is shown immediately after his stunning upset of Sonny Liston to become the heavyweight champion of the world.

Liston, after spitting out his mouthpiece, refused to get off his stool and come out for the seventh round, claiming he had hurt his shoulder.

Clay is shouting, "I am the king! I am the king! . . . Eat your words," as he taunts the many journalists sitting ringside who had doubted him, and worse.

The NOI hierarchy is structured along military lines. The troops are called the Fruit of Islam, and there are lieutenants, captains, and soldiers. Some view the sect as not merely militant but violent.

Now Cassius Clay's unexpected announcement has thrust the controversial group into the national spotlight, a light that shines harshly. There is no predicting what the results will be, although surely the previously unknown or misunderstood organization's visibility will be increased considerably.

Whether Clay's announcement is good for the NOI or the country remains to be seen. In the meantime, sportswriters and others—critics, skeptics, and so-called experts—have questioned the motives not only of the young fighter but of the Messenger, as Elijah Muhammad is called by his followers.

Clearly, the young man from Louisville has been doing some serious thinking about what it means to grow up in white America when you have black skin.

Addressing himself to the gentlemen of the press—and therefore, thanks to his new status, the nation—he said, "I know where I'm going and I know the truth, and I don't have to be what you want me to be. I'm free to be what I want."

Spoken like a true American.

And like many young Americans—white as well as black—he is searching for a light that will illuminate the way and help him navigate the deep and turbulent waters of what promises to be a decade of much upheaval and change.

suspenders, and bow ties. The women are required to have their head covered and wear white, floor-length gowns. The NOI defines women in ways that are significantly different from current mainstream definitions. The NOI has also built schools to educate their children.

THE NATIONAL HORIZON

March 6, 1964 · *When You Really Want to Know*

WHAT'S IN A NAME?
By K. D. Hesse

What's in a name? Apparently everything.

At least according to the young man from Louisville who no longer wishes to be called Cassius Clay, or even, as he announced only days ago, Cassius X (explaining that Clay was a slave owner's name and that slaves did not know their names; hence the *X*).

Now Elijah Muhammad, the spiritual leader of the Nation of Islam (NOI), has honored him with a new name: Muhammad Ali, meaning "worthy of praise."

Both parents are unhappy about this recent development and have reportedly refused to call their son by any name other than the one they gave him at birth.

In the case of Cassius Sr., the boy's father, this is a most paradoxical position. The senior Clay is unashamedly antiwhite and happy to tell anyone that race prejudice is the reason he is only a semisuccessful sign painter. No doubt his speeches on the subject were absorbed by both boys. Younger brother Rudy, who became a black Muslim even before Cassius, changed his name to Rahman Ali.

The always affable Odessa Clay is a churchgoing woman and does not subscribe to the black Muslim racist ideology. She feels that both boys have been brainwashed by a cult, and that they want Cassius because of his money. There is no doubt that Cassius Jr.'s decision has caused a rift within the family.

According to sources, Cassius Clay first became interested in the NOI when he was sixteen and traveled to Atlanta for a boxing tournament. When he subsequently went to Chicago, where the group's headquarters were located, he visited the temple and returned home with their newspaper, *Muhammad Speaks*. This winter, while in Miami training for his fight with Sonny Liston, Cassius attended meetings there as well.

Speaking to members of the NOI during a rally in Harlem in late January, he proudly proclaimed: "I'm a race man and every time I go to a Muslim meeting I get inspired."

In a newspaper interview shortly after the rally, he addressed the issue of separatism versus integration, and criticism of the NOI, in his characteristically candid manner: "Integration is wrong. The white people don't want integration, I don't want integration. I don't believe in forcing it, and the Muslims don't believe in it. So what's wrong with the Muslims?"

This, of course, is not the course advocated by the Reverend Dr. Martin Luther King Jr. Dr. King's nonviolent movement's goal is full integration into American society—in education, employment and economic opportunity, housing, access to public facilities, and culture.

He voiced this vision eloquently this past year during the March on Washington: "I have a dream that my four little children will one day live in a nation where they will not be judged by the color of their skin but by the content of their character. I have a dream today!"

The Nation of Islam has a very different vision.

Not only do they reject nonviolence, but they reject the very idea of integration. The two races, they believe, will never get along. Never be able to live harmoniously side by side. Race purity is their goal, and keeping the races separate is the means to that goal. They do not want their children going to school with white children.

Clay, referring to the recent sit-ins at whites-only lunch counters in Southern states, refuses to back off or apologize: "Should I be condemned because I refuse to put my life in jeopardy over where I can drink a cup of coffee?"

A good question.

What you people are missing about Muhammad Ali is that he's just saying what a lot of black folk in my neighborhood are thinking but are too afraid to say out loud. His courageous actions both inside and outside the ring are sending a message to Negroes all across America: Stop being afraid, stand up, and speak out. We have been Uncle Toms, bowing and scraping before the white man, for too long, and it's time to stop all that nonsense.

If Cassius Clay deciding what religion he believes in and changing his name shakes up white America, then maybe it's about time.

Thomas Preston
Minneapolis, Minnesota

I grew up my whole life hearing how white is good and black is bad, how white is superior and black inferior.

Now along comes Muhammad Ali and says, "It ain't so." Black is beautiful, just like him. He's black and he's proud of that fact, so maybe the rest of us should stop feeling sorry for ourselves and get with the program.

Very truly yours,
Miranda Collins
Roxbury, Massachusetts

---

for one, am relieved to read that
nsible journals like the *New York Times*
ot stooping so low as to call Cassius Clay
ame other than the one he was given at
by his loving parents.

ncerely,
rank L. Schaeffer
mont, New Jersey

When Gaseous Cassius isn't needlessly needling his Negro opponents before the fight, he's bragging about beating them and predicting what round they'll go in. Then during the fight he verbally insults and taunts them. I mean, how much respect can he have for his blood brothers if that's the way he treats them? It's outrageous, if you ask me, and you people in the press just lap it up, don't you?

All any of you are interested in, Clay included, is money.

Doc Chaney
Roxbury, Massachusetts

We here in Louisville have a unique understanding of Cassius Clay. We saw him rise up as a boy and win a coveted place on the U.S. Olympic team in 1960—surely a great honor! And he conducted himself with such dignity, telling that Russian TV guy how he felt about America, despite the problems, and how it was his country, right or wrong. We were so proud!

Now he goes and joins a hate group and changes his name to something no one can pronounce.

Most of us in the town he was born and raised in feel betrayed and can barely recognize the nice boy we once knew inside the mean, rude, angry young man who has replaced him.

Sincerely yours,
Eleanor Griffin
Louisville, Kentucky

Muhammad Ali is a prophet who has graciously accepted his destiny: to lead his people out of the morass in which they find themselves and on to higher ground. Like all visionaries, he will be assailed from all sides: ridiculed, criticized, vilified, and attacked at every turn.

No matter.

He will prevail in the end.

WHO IS THAT MAN?

By K. D. Hesse

In the days immediately preceding his astounding ascension to the heavyweight throne Muhammad Ali was seen around town in the company of a tall, reddish-haired, light-skinned Negro.

"Who is that man?" many people wondered.

He's known as Malcolm X.

He was born Malcolm Little in Omaha, Nebraska, in 1925, one of eight children. He spent his early teenage years in foster homes and then worked odd jobs.

By the time Malcolm was seventeen, he was drifting back and forth between Boston and New York, selling drugs. Four years later Big Red was arrested, convicted, and sent to prison, where he embarked on a self-education program and decided to join the Nation of Islam.

When Malcolm was paroled in 1952, Elijah Muhammad, the leader of the Nation of Islam, made him the head of the Detroit mosque. Muhammad then moved him to Mosque No. 7, in Harlem.

Malcolm X proved to be a highly effective organizer and evangelical recruiter. The recent dramatic rise in membership is due, in large part, to his efforts.

Malcolm has gained a reputation in recent years as someone who tells it like it is. To people who say the black Muslims are advocating violence, he responds: "We're nonviolent with people who are nonviolent with us."

Cassius Clay first heard Malcolm X speak in 1960 when he was visiting New York City immediately after his Olympic victory in Rome. Two years later, in 1962, when the up-and-coming fighter visited Detroit, he introduced himself to Malcolm X. They took a liking to each other and over the following months spent some time together and their friendship blossomed.

Clay even invited Malcolm and his family to come to Miami, where he was living while he trained for his big fight against Liston. In many ways Malcolm X inspired the young fighter and acted as his guru. They all celebrated the fighter's twenty-second birthday on January 17 with a cake topped by a sugar version of Clay standing over a defeated Sonny Liston, arms overhead, celebrating the victory.

Immediately after the fight Clay passed up a party at the Fontainebleau Hotel and headed back to the Hampton House Motel, where Malcolm X offered one of his typically provocative opinions: "Clay is the finest Negro athlete I have ever known, the man who will come to mean more to his people than Jackie Robinson . . . because Robinson is the white man's hero. But Cassius is the black man's hero." The celebration was topped off, ironically, by vanilla ice cream.

MISSING
CALL FBI

THE FBI IS SEEKING INFORMATION CONCERNING THE DISAPPEARANCE AT PHILADELPHIA, MISSISSIPPI, OF THESE THREE INDIVIDUALS ON JUNE 21, 1964. EXTENSIVE INVESTIGATION IS BEING CONDUCTED TO LOCATE GOODMAN, CHANEY, AND SCHWERNER, WHO ARE DESCRIBED AS FOLLOWS:

ANDREW GOODMAN **JAMES EARL CHANEY** **MICHAEL HENRY SCHWERNER**

RACE:	White	Negro	White
SEX:	Male	Male	Male
DOB:	November 23, 1943	May 30, 1943	November 6, 1939
POB:	New York City	Meridian, Mississippi	New York City
AGE:	20 years	21 years	24 years
HEIGHT:	5'10"	5'7"	5'9" to 5'10"
WEIGHT:	150 pounds	135 to 140 pounds	170 to 180 pounds
HAIR:	Dark brown; wavy	Black	Brown
EYES:	Brown	Brown	Light blue
TEETH:		Good: none missing	
SCARS AND MARKS:		1 inch cut scar 2 inches above left ear.	Pock mark center of forehead, slight scar on bridge of nose, appendectomy scar, broken leg scar.

SHOULD YOU HAVE OR IN THE FUTURE RECEIVE ANY INFORMATION CONCERNING THE WHEREABOUTS OF THESE INDIVIDUALS, YOU ARE REQUESTED TO NOTIFY ME OR THE NEAREST OFFICE OF THE FBI. TELEPHONE NUMBER IS LISTED BELOW.

DIRECTOR
FEDERAL BUREAU OF INVESTIGATION
UNITED STATES DEPARTMENT OF JUSTICE
WASHINGTON, D. C. 20535
TELEPHONE, NATIONAL 8-7117

, 1964

Civil Rights Workers Missing

On Sunday, June 21, 1964, in Philadelphia, Mississippi, three civil rights workers—Michael Schwerner, 24, Andrew Goodman, 20 (both white and from the New York City area), and James Chaney, 21 (a local Negro)—were reported missing.

All three were participating in Freedom Summer, a project aimed at helping Mississippi's colored residents register to vote, get better jobs, and improve their education. The men were last seen at a church that had been burned to the ground by a group of white men looking for Michael Schwerner, who wanted to establish a Freedom School there.

After the charred chassis of their Ford Fairlane station wagon was discovered in a swamp, the FBI offered a reward for information. There was an anonymous tip that led federal authorities to a huge earthen dam where the three bodies were found.

The search, which drew intense national attention, even from the president, had lasted forty-four days.

All three men had been shot at close range with a single weapon.

Malcolm X Assassinated! Dies Instantly
Three Gunmen, One Apprehended

February 21, 1965

Speaking at a rally before his newly formed Organization of Afro-American Unity in late June last year, Malcolm X stated: "We want freedom by any means necessary. We want justice by any means necessary. We want equality by any means necessary."

Apparently, his enemies subscribed to a similar philosophy.

Eyewitnesses of the assassination report that there were three gunmen involved and that one was apprehended at the scene—the Audubon Ballroom in Washington Heights, north of Harlem, in New York City. There are further, unconfirmed reports that the Nation of Islam (NOI) was involved.

The day before he was assassinated, Malcolm X told photographer Gordon Parks, "It's a time for martyrs now, and if I am to be one, it will be in the cause of brotherhood."

At one time Malcolm X was considered not only the highest-ranking minister in the Nation of Islam but the heir apparent to Elijah Muhammad. Apparently, their relationship began to deteriorate after Malcolm's controversial remarks about the Kennedy assassination while delivering a speech in New York City entitled "God's Judgement of White America." In a Q-and-A period that followed the speech Malcolm responded to a reporter's query about the events in Dallas, saying it was a case of "the chickens coming home to roost" and adding that "being an old farm boy myself, chickens coming home to roost never made me sad; they've always made me glad." Malcolm X made these inflammatory comments even though Elijah Muhammad, well aware of the nation's intense emotional connection to the suddenly slain president, had ordered all ministers to refrain from making any comment on the tragic event and had personally phoned Malcolm to deliver the message.

Not only did Malcolm X's comments outrage white Americans and alienate him further from conservative Negroes, but since he defied Elijah Muhammad's direct order to remain silent on the events of November 22, 1963, his comments served to further widen the growing split between the two men.

That split, according to confidential sources, had as much to do with jealousy as anything else. Malcolm's oratorical skills, which led to speaking engagements at numerous prestigious universities, his popularity with urban Negroes, who saw him as pointing the way to the future, and his favored status with the white media were all perceived by Elijah Muhammad as threats to his leadership.

In addition, Malcolm had been critical of Elijah Muhammad's ethics and had been evolving his own philosophy away from the racist, whites-as-blue-eyed-devils NOI ideology to a more inclusive brotherhood-of-man concept. In March 1964 he announced he was leaving the NOI and forming his own organization. Knowledgeable sources tell us that Malcolm was hoping his protégé, Muhammad Ali, would join him. That is not to be, however: Ali has shunned his former mentor and sided with Elijah Muhammad.

Recently Ali told an interviewer: "You don't just buck Mr. Muhammad and get away with it. I don't want to talk about [Malcolm] no more."

Malcolm X was thirty-nine.

November 14, 1964

Clay Rushed to Hospital

Incarcerated Inguinal Hernia
Taken on Stretcher
Surgery Successful
Liston Rematch Postponed

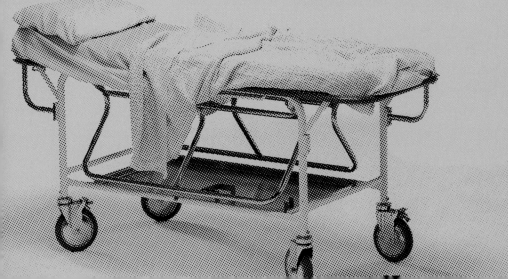

VIETNAM

In late March 1964, Muhammad Ali (as he was becoming known) failed the mental aptitude part of the army's qualifying exam. He was declared 1-Y, meaning he was unlikely to be drafted.

At that time there were approximately twenty-five thousand American military advisers in Vietnam.

Ten months later, in early January 1965, this photo was taken in a small village only forty miles east of Saigon, the South Vietnamese capital. That the Vietcong had infiltrated that far south came as a surprise. In the six-day battle that ensued five Americans were killed and three wounded—the highest total for a single battle in Vietnam to that point.

By the end of the year there were 180,000 American soldiers

THE BIGGER THEY COME, THE HARDER THEY FALL

ALI VS. LISTON II

By Keith Kincaid

Maybe it was the last-minute venue change of the already hernia-postponed bout to very out-of-the-way Lewiston, Maine (pop. 41,000).

Or it could have been the site: a hockey "arena" used mostly by kids with a seating capacity of, get this, 5,500.

But mostly it was the rumor.

Malcolm X's followers were coming to avenge his death by killing Muhammad Ali, who had not only severed all communications with his friend and former mentor but sided with Elijah Muhammad. As a result the new champion was surrounded at all times by serious-looking members of the Fruit of Islam, the militant wing of the Nation of Islam.

Like Ali, the town's police chief wasn't taking any chances: "I don't want to go down in history as the place where the heavyweight champion was killed." Security was beefed up with uniformed and plainclothes police, and all handbags and briefcases were searched as people entered the arena.

The *Boston Globe* was taking no chances either; they took out extra insurance on all the writers assigned to cover the fight.

To say that the atmosphere was tense and everyone was on edge would be a vast understatement.

And the fight didn't help any.

Wasting not a moment, Ali marched out of his corner and smacked a surprised Sonny Liston with a straight right. Of course, if Liston had listened to Ali in the weeks before the fight when he told reporters how the opening strategy had come to him in a recurring dream, he would have been expecting it. Now he was entering his own nightmare.

Liston launched one of his lunging lefts. Ali, who has greater hand and foot speed than any heavyweight in recent memory, moved just far enough out of the way to avoid the punch and shot a perfectly timed right cross over Liston's limp, fully extended arm, simultaneously pivoting on his right foot to add a little extra strength to the hit. Ali caught Liston on the side of his head, snapping it back. The punch packed so much power that it lifted Liston's firmly planted left foot off the canvas.

As every boxing maven knows, it's the punch you *don't* see coming that gets you. It's the mental shock not the physical power, and Sonny Liston never saw it coming.

Liston went down like a building had fallen on him, managed to get to his hands and knees, and then rolled over onto his back. The ref, who seemed at least as confused as Liston, waited an eternity before starting the count. It didn't really matter—you had the feeling he could have counted to a million and Liston wasn't going to part with the canvas.

The crowd began yelling, "Fix! Fix!"

You couldn't really blame them. Since the crowd was just settling into the arena, and Ali had thrown less than a handful of punches, most hadn't seen much of the fight at all, and before anyone could say "down for the count," Liston was.

Those who *had* seen the punch, however, were just plain angry that their fun was over in two minutes and twelve seconds.

Meanwhile, the nearly hysterical victor, who hadn't bothered to go to a neutral corner, was standing over his sprawling victim shouting: "Get up and fight, you bum! You're supposed to be so bad! Nobody will believe this!"

He's right. Nobody did.

Liston went down like a tree. As they say, the bigger the come, the harder they fall.

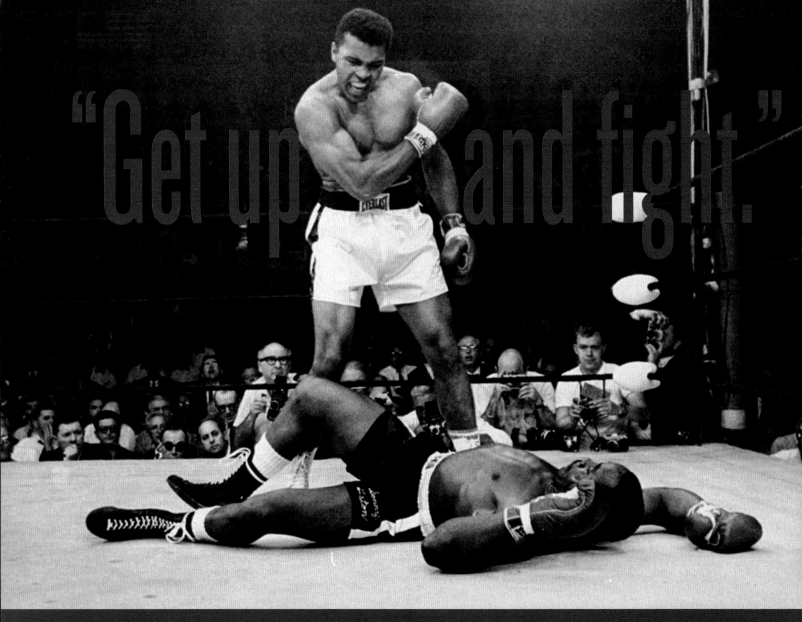

"Get up and fight."

Fifteen months earlier Cassius Clay stunned the boxing world by defeating Sonny Liston.

Nearly as surprising was his KO of Liston in two minutes and twelve seconds of the first round of their May 25, 1965, rematch.

Here Clay, then known as Muhammad Ali, is shouting: "Get up and fight, you bum! You're supposed to be so bad! Nobody will believe this!"

"PHANTOM PUNCH" KO'S LISTON

CLAY RETAINS TITLE

In Ring Anecdote, Clay Says Patterson Can Have the Heavyweight Title

Patterson Condemns Muslims

Says They Preach Hate ... KKK

Clay Vows to Punish ...

Clay ... Scared Rabbit

... and Carrots to His Training Camp

Patterson Promises to Reclaim Title

WHAT'S RACE GOT TO DO WITH IT?

By Keith Kincaid

The new heavyweight champion of the world, unlike some others I could name, has already shown an admirable take-on-all-comers approach by offering former title holder Floyd Patterson a shot.

Patterson doesn't take a backseat to anyone when it comes to being strange—some writers we know refer to him as Freud Patterson, while others (of a particular thespian bent) prefer "the Heavyweight Hamlet."

He decided to thank Muhammad Ali for this opportunity to regain the crown by writing not one but two not-so-nice articles denouncing him for joining a racist organization and being a disgrace to the world of boxing. Patterson promised to regain the title for America, and it wasn't long before things settled down to some good old-fashioned name-calling (dutifully recorded by the press). Patterson said taking the title away from Clay (as he insists on and persists in calling him) was a "moral crusade," so Ali countered by calling Patterson "a white man's Negro." Or vice versa, it's hard to keep track.

Ali first met Patterson back in 1960 when he was an eighteen-year-old gold medal winner named Cassius Clay and Patterson was touring the Olympic village as the reigning champ. An excited Clay ran up to Patterson and stuck out his hand. When a distracted Patterson could barely take the time to press the flesh, Clay—who even back then was not someone who forgot a slight (especially from folks he eventually met back in the ring)—took note.

Now Ali has promised to "punish" Patterson for his remarks.

Once upon a time prizefighters were supposed to answer only softball questions with words of one syllable: How ya doin', champ? Are ya rested? Who ya takin' on next?

Now it's: Why'd you join that racist group? Who do you think you are, changing your name? What do you think about integration?

Discussions about race and racism, which are becoming with each passing day more and more a part of daily life, are now becoming a part of boxing. For better or for worse, who's to say?

One thing's for certain: Muhammad Ali is the reason.

PUNISHING PATTERSON

WILL THE REAL MUHAMMAD ALI PLEASE STAND UP?

By Keith Kincaid

Did someone once say, "It is a riddle wrapped in a mystery inside an enigma"?

Whoever did must have had Muhammad Ali in mind.

A year ago, when Ali first turned the usually boring boxing world on its collective thick skull with back-to-back Sonny Liston fights (although some of my more conservative colleagues refuse to apply that term to their second encounter), the Ali act was relatively new, especially if you hadn't followed his post-Olympic/early amateur career.

Since then we have learned that, like the magician who doesn't want to reveal how he does the trick, Ali doesn't want you to think he works at it. But he does.

In fact, not only was "Listonmania" not spontaneous, it was the result of hours spent talking to people who knew Liston and watching his behavior closely. Very closely. And Ali was taking notes—mental notes so he could conjure up his bizarre game plan like the alchemist he is.

Once Ali figured out how Liston's mind worked, he was able to get inside it. Those seemingly spontaneous hysterical rants were purposely designed to convince Liston that Ali was not only crazy—and therefore capable of anything—but a clown who didn't have to be taken seriously. The fight was won before the opening bell.

Which brings us to last night's fight, when Ali, as promised, punished Floyd Patterson for twelve painful rounds, relieved only when the ref took a moment to warn the champion to stop all the jawing. Fat chance. It was, in fact, cruel and unusual punishment, and many reporters believe (present company not included) that Ali refrained from knocking Patterson out to prolong the pain. Of course, Patterson's refusal to go down didn't help matters.

Truth was, Patterson didn't belong inside the same ring as Ali. Not on this night. Not on any night.

But we're more interested in what happened right *after* the fight, when Ali and Patterson dutifully consented to a ringside interview. That's when we saw the mask drop, just for a minute or two. We'd seen it before. In a brief moment at the very end of Liston I, after Clay had finished shouting at the nonbelievers in press row that now they had to eat their words. Surprisingly, and coaxed by no one, he went over to the man he had just defeated and gave him a consoling pat on the back. Curious, we thought, How does that fit into the act?

During the Ali/Patterson postfight interview Ali seemed eager to give his adversary his due. He said he was surprised at how many punches Patterson could take, and admitted he was wrong about how soon Patterson would fall. Ali told Patterson he respected him for not going down. He was, Ali said, a real man.

We thought maybe this was part of the Ali act and the punch line was just around the corner. But it wasn't. Fighting twelve rounds will do that to you. Peel away some of the layers. Make you drop the mask and reveal the truth, if only for a brief, shining moment.

Honest, straightforward, respectful, humble. Muhammad Ali.

But that doesn't sell tickets or fill seats, and we suspect that the various masks—the loudmouth, the clown, the poet, the angry young Negro, and all the others—in Ali's seemingly limitless arsenal will, in the coming weeks, reappear. And they will once again obscure the real person that this writer suspects is behind the masks as the undefeated heavyweight champion of the world prepares for his next opponent.

"Why me?"

February 17, 1966

Muhammad Ali is seen on the lawn outside the house he is renting in Miami, Florida. He has just learned from a reporter that the draft board in his hometown—Louisville, Kentucky—has reclassified him I-A.

This means he is eligible to be drafted immediately and possibly sent to fight in the escalating war in Vietnam.

He is surrounded by kids in the neighborhood and is saying, "Why me?"

2:00 p.m.
CLAY DECLARED ELIGIBLE FOR DRAFT

Reported by Nick Paglia

Good evening.

Nick Paglia here, outside Cassius Clay's residence, bringing you the latest news concerning his sudden draft status change.

Earlier today Clay received a call from a reporter who told him he was no longer I-Y (meaning his service in the military was deferred) and had been reclassified I-A (meaning he could be drafted immediately).

We are surrounded by reporters, photographers, cameramen, and sound trucks not only from local radio and TV stations but from the networks.

First, some background:

Six years ago, shortly after his eighteenth birthday, Clay, as required by law, registered for the draft in his hometown of Louisville, Kentucky. Four years later, after failing the mental aptitude test (he had no problem with the physical part), he was classified I-Y. At the time he laughed it off, quipping to reporters, "I said I was the greatest, not the smartest."

In 1960 most Americans hadn't even heard of Vietnam; there were only seven hundred military advisers stationed there. Now, six years later, there are 185,000 American soldiers fighting in South Vietnam. In response to President Johnson's decision to widen the war—meaning even more ground troops would be needed—the draft rolls had to be increased. Military authorities have therefore lowered the minimum acceptable score on the mental aptitude test from thirty down to fifteen. Clay's score

was sixteen, meaning he is now, by one point, qualified to serve in the military.

Needless to say, this afternoon's news came as quite a shock to the usually unflappable fighter. Clearly agitated, not only by the constant phone calls from reporters but the barrage of questions from the ones on the scene (including this reporter), Clay began to respond with uncharacteristic confusion and frustration. Finally, at one point, he appeared to have lost

patience entirely when a reporter asked if he even knew where Vietnam was or who the Vietcong were.

"I ain't got nothing against them Vietcong," Clay declared.

I am sure this remark will provide us with not only tomorrow's headlines but the beginning of yet another controversy in a career that seems to court controversy.

This is Nick Paglia, reporting live for WLTN, Miami, Florida.

SPORTSWORLD WEEKLY

The Peanut Gallery

By Keith Kincaid

As we all know by now, Muhammad Ali—never one to shy away from a topic (no matter how hot it is or how unqualified he is)—has issued his somewhat spontaneous, certainly provocative, and charmingly succinct position paper on the war in Vietnam.

"Man, I ain't got no quarrel with them Vietcong" was how he put it.

Naturally, the nation's venerable stable of sportswriters and former boxing greats have circled the wagons in hopes of protecting the soul of America. And what better way of doing that than punishing anyone who is out of step with their "America—love it or leave it, and certainly don't disagree with it" mentality.

Here's just a small sampling of what they've had to say:

> Squealing over the possibility that the military may call him up, Cassius makes himself as sorry a spectacle as those unwashed punks who picket and demonstrate against the war.
>
> —Red Smith, *New York Herald Tribune*

> As a fighter, Cassius is good. As a man, he cannot compare to some of those kids slogging through the rice paddies where the names are stranger than Muhammad Ali.
>
> —Milton Gross, *New York Post*

> For his stomach-turning performance, boxing should throw Clay out on his inflated head. The adult brat, who has boasted ad nauseam of his fighting skill but who squealed like a cornered rat when tapped for the Army, should be shorn of his title. And to the devil with the old cliché that a ring title can be won or lost only in the ring.
>
> —Murray Robinson, *New York Journal-American*

> Clay is part of the Beatle movement. He fits in with the famous singers no one can hear and punks riding motorcycles with iron crosses pinned to their leather jackets and Batman and the boys with their long dirty hair and the girls with the unwashed look and the college kids dancing naked at secret proms held in apartments and the revolt of students who get a check from Dad every first of the month and the painters who copy the labels off soup cans and the surf bums who refuse to work and the whole pampered style-making cult of the bored young.
>
> —Jimmy Cannon, *New York Journal-American*

> This benighted fellow . . . mistakes crowds and headlines as approval of himself. But the day of reckoning will not go away and inexorably in his future is jail as a draft dodger . . . What he knows is that he is an attraction, wherever he goes, even more so since he festooned his heavyweight title with the label of No. 1 draft evader.
>
> —Shirley Povich, *Washington Post*

> Muhammad Ali is finished as a fighter. Regardless of the outcome of his next fight, he is finished. He should be careful. It's not safe for him to be on the streets.
>
> —Former heavyweight champion Jack Dempsey

> You have disgraced your title and the American flag and the principles for which it stands. Apologize for your unpatriotic remarks or you'll be barred from the ring.
>
> —Former heavyweight champion Gene Tunney in a telegram to Ali

Terrible Terrell

By Keith Kincaid

Muhammad Ali—whom other sportswriters, certain ring announcers, and almost every TV commentator insist on calling Cassius Clay—has, as we know, lately been battling politicians and the Pentagon.

We sometimes forget that he actually fights other boxers from time to time. Does quite well at it, as a matter of fact. As he says: "It's just a job. Grass grows, birds fly, waves pound the sand. I beat people up."

Last year he fought and defeated five serious contenders, and four of his five wins were KOs. The last, three months ago, was against a tough customer named Cleveland Williams. Ali—who, according to some so-called experts, supposedly can't throw a punch with power—knocked Williams down four times in three rounds, winning a TKO in the third.

Ernie Terrell, his most recent opponent, was thought to be another, even more formidable foe. But the bout was about politics as well as fisticuffs. Terrell, like Floyd Patterson, has refused to call the champ by his nom de choice.

Bad choice.

"I really feel sorry for Clay. . . . It is wrong and harmful to promote religion or politics with your championship," Terrell said.

Then he compared Ali to Hitler and the devil. Ali comforted himself by calling Terrell an "Uncle Tom."

Ali stated with characteristic prefight bravado, "I want to torture him. A clean knockout is too good for him."

He did, and it was.

The fourth was Terrible Terrell's only good round, and that, barely. In the eighth, knowing he had nothing to fear, Ali taunted Terrell repeatedly just like he did Patterson: "What's my name?" he inquired between jabs that were causing one of Terrell's eyes to swell closed. By the twelfth Angelo Dundee was begging his fighter to finish it. The fat cats at ringside agreed, screaming for the ref to stop the fight.

Ali was, as usual, untouched.

Some, I'm sure, will call the fight vicious, brutal, and cruel. And they'd be right.

Problem is, fighting *is* vicious, brutal, and cruel. Terrell *was* a formidable foe, and Ali was able to toy with him. Ali's snakelike left jab is—although traveling only a short distance—deceptively punishing. To paraphrase Dundee: "People forget a jab's still a punch to the face." Unusual for a heavyweight, he has hand and foot speed not seen since Sugar Ray Robinson, who was a middleweight. Add to this his uncanny reflexes, his underrated ability to take a punch, and his ever-vigilant eyes, which allow him to see the ring at all times.

Fact is, Muhammad Ali, like him or not, combines the best of Jack Johnson and Joe Louis. Like Johnson, Ali has size, grace, and balance. Both use an unorthodox defensive style, jerking their heads back just far enough out of harm's way—and at the very last moment. Either man could launch a devastating counterattack when his opponent let down his guard. And both seemed to enjoy taunting their adversaries.

Of course quiet, gentlemanly Joe Louis was their opposite as a fighter and a man. But Ali's fast hands and ability to punch accurately with power remind many seasoned observers of the Brown Bomber himself.

Add it all up and you have the best heavyweight boxer of our time.

There's only one foe on the horizon that is capable of taking that away from him: the United States government.

VIETNAM: THE LOGIC OF WITHDRAWAL

Two months after Muhammad Ali learned he was eligible to be drafted, Boston University history professor Howard Zinn—an early and outspoken critic of the war—addressed an antiwar rally on the MIT campus in Cambridge, Massachusetts.

That same year Zinn published *Vietnam: The Logic of Withdrawal*. He was one of the first, if not *the* first, important voices to declare the war unjust and to advocate that the United States withdraw unconditionally and immediately.

By the end of 1967 the antiwar movement had gained momentum, as 100,000 marched in the nation's capital and 400,000 in New York City. For the first time polls showed that most Americans opposed the war.

THE STEP

July 4, 1967

Independence Day seemed like an appropriate time to review the events that have unfolded this past year in the case of the always controversial Muhammad Ali.

In mid-March 1966—a month after hearing that he had been reclassified 1-A—Muhammad Ali went before the Louisville draft board and stated that he could not serve in the army for two reasons: One, the financial hardship it would cause his parents due to his loss of boxing income. And two, he was a conscientious objector based on his religion, Islam.

The board denied his request.

Ali, the Justice Department said, had two choices: be inducted into the army or go to jail as a draft evader.

In April of this year he received a notice to report to the Houston induction center (he was, by then, living in Houston).

Before he left for the induction center, Ali spoke on the phone with his mother, who said: "Do the right thing. If I were you, I would go ahead and take the step. If I were you, I would join the Army. Do you understand me, son?"

Although her son did, indeed, understand her, he had no intention of taking "the step" she wanted him to take.

"Mama, I love you," he replied. "Whatever I do, Mama, remember I love you."

Ali did report to the induction center on the date requested, and a navy officer escorted Ali into a large room, where he joined thirty other draftees (he was the only one without an overnight bag). First they had their physical examination. Next the inductees ate lunch together. Then they were told to march down the hall to a smaller room. They all lined up. The room was quiet.

The group was ordered to stand at attention. An officer explained that when their name was called, they should take a step forward, signifying that they

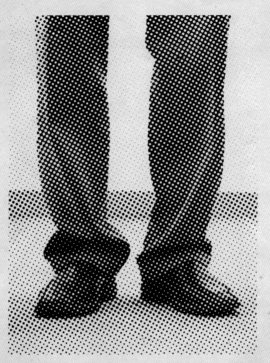

were willing to enter the military. He began calling out the names.

Ali's former name, Cassius Clay, was called.

The room was silent. Ali did not move. The officer stood in front of Ali and stared at him. He called his name again. This time he said: "Cassius Clay, will you please step forward and be inducted into the armed forces of the United States?"

Ali did not move. Another officer came into the room and escorted Ali to a nearby office. There the officer explained to him that he might be charged with a crime and face five years in jail and a $10,000 fine if he refused to be inducted. The officer asked Ali if he would like to change his mind, and Ali said he would not. He signed a statement about his reasons for refusing service in the military and then left.

As Ali came out of the induction center, the military police had a difficult time controlling the crowds and TV cameras gathered outside. The reporters shouted at Ali, asking what he had done.

One reporter asked if Ali was willing to take the consequences of his actions. Ali told him, "Every day they die in Vietnam for nothing. I might as well die right here for something." Asked by another reporter if he, like many draft dodgers, would move to Canada, Ali replied, "America is my birth country. They make the rules, and if they want to put me in jail, I'll go to jail. But I'm an American and I'm not running away."

It was a long day, but he still had a phone call to make.

"Mama," he said, "I'm all right. I did what I had to do. I sure am looking forward to coming home to eat some of your cooking."

The chairman of the New York State Athletic Commission said that Ali's beliefs were "detrimental to the best interests of boxing." The commission took away his license to box in New York State. Other states quickly followed, and in no time Ali was unable to get a license to box anywhere in the country.

Muhammad Ali was charged with refusing to serve in the armed forces of the United States. He pleaded not guilty. When Ali's case reached the federal court, his lawyers gave three reasons why Ali was asking to be excused from military service: His religion did not allow him to fight in a war not approved by Allah (the Islamic word for God); he was a practicing minister, and ministers were not drafted; and as a black man, he could not fight against the dark-skinned people of Vietnam.

In June the Justice Department found Muhammad Ali guilty of draft evasion. He was fined $10,000 and given the maximum sentence: five years in prison. But he has not gone to jail because his lawyers are planning to appeal the case, taking it to a more powerful court and arguing the case there, hoping for an outcome in Ali's favor.

CONTROVERSIAL BOXER WEDS

Former heavyweight champion Cassius Clay, twenty-five, married seventeen-year-old Belinda Boyd in a small, private ceremony yesterday.

The couple first met in 1960 when the up-and-coming fighter spoke during an assembly at her Muslim school. Belinda Boyd, who was eleven at the time, was a top student and worked on the school newspaper.

Clay was previously married for two years to Sonji Roi. They were divorced in 1966. Court papers say that Clay claimed she had promised to become a Muslim but failed to keep that promise.

It's like *Alice's Adventures in Wonderland*: "Sentence first—verdict afterwards."

They take away his title, and then every state in the union announces they don't want him fighting in their backyards—all this before he's convicted of anything. Actually, before he's even charged with anything.

What happened to "innocent until proven guilty"? What happened to due process?

Oh yes, I forgot, that's for white folks.

Now, after all this time, his appeal is rejected, and they not only fine him $10,000 and sentence him to five years in jail—the max, by the way—but take away his license and revoke his passport. Nice. So now he can't fight inside his own country, and he can't leave and go fight somewhere else.

Basically they just took away the man's ability to earn a living.

Where's the justice in that?

What's being done to Muhammad Ali is a crime, pure and simple.

Septima Chandler
Teacher, Poet, Negro
Chicago, Illinois

It is the patriotic duty of every American male, including Cassius Clay, to serve in the military if his country calls.

All this bunk about him not being able to support his mommy and daddy (and keep them all in Cadillacs) is just a bunch of junk, and anyone with half a brain knows it. He's got plenty of money from those Liston fights, and he didn't even have to work up a sweat. He just fought Terrell in the Astrodome and set an indoor attendance record—how much chump change did the champ get for that?

My boy had to leave behind a good job right here in town because he felt obliged to defend his country. Right or wrong.

And he didn't wait to be drafted—he enlisted. Now he's stationed in Da Nang, Vietnam, and I'm damned proud of him.

Clay's no better than my boy. As a matter of fact, as far as I'm concerned, he's a shameless traitor and, worse, a coward.

The only place for him is behind bars, which appears to be precisely where he's headed.

Mark Wright
Wright and Sons Stationers
Nashville, Tennessee

Ali is simply saying what a lot of people are thinking. Once again he's just ahead of his time—like he was back in '64.

Anyone who reads the papers or watches the nightly news—and that includes Ali—knows that "American boys" are coming home in body bags as the body count rises each week. Of course, the equally innocent Asian boys and girls are busy searching through the wreckage for the bodies of their parents, killed by bombs they cannot see or hear.

Most Americans are only now coming to realize what is going on over there.

Ali is guilty of only one thing: speaking the truth. The government is just trying to silence him.

Daniel Lewis
Professor of History
Cambridge, Massachusetts

Everyone seems mystified by Muhammad Ali's recent decision not to be inducted into the army. But he's made it quite clear why he's chosen the path he has:

"Why should they ask me, another so-called Negro, to put on a uniform and go ten thousand miles from home and drop bombs and bullets on brown people in Vietnam, while so-called Negro people in Louisville are treated like dogs and denied simple human rights?"

Simple question and one more people should be asking themselves.

Lucy Robinson
Housewife
Louisville, Kentucky

He sure seems to bring out the worst in people.

He's a hero.

He's a villain.

No one seems to consider the idea that he's a scared young man—only twenty-six, I think—and being confronted with decisions that no young man should be confronted with. No one seems to consider the idea that perhaps he's not really sure what to do and is doing the best he can in an extremely complicated situation.

And no one seems to think he deserves a little more of our sympathy and a little less of our scorn. Especially from those of us who consider ourselves adults.

Bob Mills
Retired
Boca Raton, Florida

"The Mountaintop"

On April 4, 1968, Dr. Martin Luther King Jr., thirty-nine, was assassinated while standing on the balcony of a hotel in Memphis, Tennessee. Dr. King was in Memphis supporting the local sanitation workers strike.

The night before, acutely aware of the threats on his life, he delivered a sermon that ended:

Well, I don't know what will happen now. We've got some difficult days ahead. But it really doesn't matter with me now, because I've been to the mountaintop. And I don't mind. Like anybody, I would like to live a long life. Longevity has its place. But I'm not concerned about that now. I just want to do God's will. And He's allowed me to go up to the mountain, and I've looked over, and I've seen the promised land. I may not get there with you. But I want you to know tonight that we, as a people, will get to the promised land. And so I'm happy tonight. I'm not worried about anything. I'm not fearing any man. Mine eyes have seen the glory of the coming of the Lord.

Coretta Scott King is shown here at his funeral on April 9 in Atlanta.

RFK

On March 31, 1968 (four days before Martin Luther King Jr. was assassinated), President Johnson announced he would not seek reelection. His decision was prompted by the unexpected North Vietnamese Tet Offensive earlier in the year; antiwar candidate Senator Eugene McCarthy's strong showing in the New Hampshire Democratic primary; and New York senator, and former attorney general, Robert F. Kennedy's decision to enter the race also.

In early June RFK won the important California primary. He is seen here (with his wife) just after midnight on June 5 congratulating his campaign workers. He ended the brief speech by promising to bring peace in Vietnam.

Moments later, while walking through the hotel's kitchen pantry on his way to a press conference, he was fatally wounded.

The Revolt of the Black Athlete

Runners Tommie Smith (center) and John Carlos (right) raise their arms and gloved fists in protest during the playing of "The Star-Spangled Banner" at the Mexico City Olympics on October 16, 1968. Smith won the gold and Carlos the bronze in the 200 meters. Australian silver medalist Peter Norman is wearing the same badge as Smith and Carlos to show solidarity.

The badge symbolized the organization conceived by San Jose State College professor Harry Edwards that gave rise to the revolt of the black athlete.

Edwards considered Muhammad Ali the father of the revolt (and made the reinstatement of his title and license to box his number one demand) because his actions changed the role of the black athlete in America.

Kent State

On April 30, 1970, President Nixon announced that American soldiers had invaded Cambodia, a country neighboring Vietnam.

The escalation of the already controversial war caused students on campuses across the country to demonstrate their opposition. In Ohio the governor called out the National Guard and ordered them to restore order on the campus of Kent State University.

At noon on May 4 guardsmen advanced on a group of protesters who had refused to disperse. Provoked by the rock-throwing students, the nervous National Guardsmen opened fire.

Four students were killed and several wounded.

By 1970 antiwar sentiment across America was spreading: A majority of the population now believed the war was a mistake.

In February, *Esquire* ran a cover story headlined, WE BELIEVE THAT MUHAMMAD ALI, HEAVYWEIGHT CHAMPION OF THE WORLD, SHOULD BE ALLOWED TO DEFEND HIS TITLE. It was signed by a long list of well-known names—including former critics of Ali's actions.

In late October of that year Muhammad Ali stepped into the ring for the first time in three and half years.

And on June 28, 1971, the U.S. Supreme Court unanimously voted to overturn Ali's conviction.

THE NATIONAL HORIZON

September 22, 1970 · *When You Really Want to Know*

ALI IN EXILE: PART ONE
NO GOOD DEED GOES UNPUNISHED

By K. D. Hesse

For the past three and a half years Muhammad Ali has been banned from participating in the sport he single-handedly reinvented. As the saying goes, "No good deed goes unpunished."

California's outspoken governor, Ronald Reagan (in a clear case of the pot calling the kettle black—all puns intended), spoke for the other forty-nine states when he said: "That draft dodger will never fight in my state, period." Reagan did not mention that he spent World War II stateside, making B movies with his unit—"the celluloid commandos."

Ali's legal appeal is currently crawling through the courts—justice, being blind, moves ever so slowly. So the boy who didn't pay much attention to his studies in school because he had the preposterous notion that he was going to become the heavyweight champion of the world—and therefore spent every waking minute training—now has to find another occupation. Pronto.

According to sources, the millions he made in the three years between beating Sonny Liston and beating the draft are all but gone, spent on his extravagant lifestyle, taxes, handouts to hangers-on, and support for his ex-wife, Sonji Roi, in the amount of $150,000.

Forced to take work where he could find it, the champ picked up some walking-around money when Random House coughed up $250,000 for his autobiography. He also did a documentary called *A.k.a. Cassius Clay* and starred in a not-so-great 1969 Broadway play called *Buck White*, based on the life of black heavyweight champion Jack Johnson. For $10,000 and a percentage he agreed to fight, sort of, former undefeated heavyweight champ Rocky Marciano, retired now for over a decade. The computerized fight had Marciano knocking out Ali in the thirteenth round.

A paid appearance that same year on ABC-TV's *Wide World of Sports* with his new sidekick Howard Cosell resulted in some serious difficulty for Ali. Responding to a question from Cosell, Ali admitted that, if the money was right, he would be willing to return to the ring. To most this seemed like a sane answer from a boxer in need of cash. But to Elijah Muhammad, leader of the black Muslims, this implication was inappropriate, as was participation in all sports—especially boxing.

Of course, when Ali was king of the world, and was bringing home the bacon—and donating who knows how much of it to the black Muslims—Elijah Muhammad was willing to look the other way. But now that Ali was no longer king—and indeed, down and out—he was no longer useful (or profitable), and Elijah Muhammad suspended him from the organization.

"We tell the world we're not with Muhammad Ali," read his statement in the black Muslim newspaper.

Ali accepted his punishment stoically.

One has to wonder, however, if Ali's banishment from the black Muslims didn't cause him to reflect on Malcom X's conflict with Elijah Muhammad. Did Ali regret the way he treated Malcolm, his friend and mentor?

ALI IN EXILE: PART TWO
"JUST LIKE ... ONE OF THOSE SLEEPY-LOOKIN' SENATORS"
By K. D. Hesse

Ali spent most of his time—and made most of his (non–Random House) money—speaking on college campuses across the country.

Much had changed since he blurted out his now-infamous Vietcong remark in 1966 and, a year later, refused to fight in what he considered an immoral war.

In 1968 the North Vietnamese launched the Tet Offensive, which convinced many Americans that, despite government assurances to the contrary, there was no "light at the end of the tunnel" (as they had been told), but the tunnel was in the so-called enemy's hands. The war's morality was one question. Whether it could be won or not was another. And it was starting to look like this was a war the United States could not win.

That same year a sitting president announced he would not seek a second term; civil rights leader Martin Luther King Jr. and antiwar candidate Robert Kennedy were assassinated; and the Democrats held their convention in Chicago, where Mayor Daley's police clubbed, beat, and teargassed demonstrators while the networks' news cameras beamed the horrific display into the homes of 230 million Americans.

The antiwar movement, which was a whisper when Ali first spoke out, had, by the time of the convention, become a roar that could be heard on the streets of Chicago. The whole world was watching. Soon not-so-radical citizens—housewives, blue-collar workers, and businessmen—were joining the students, professors, clergy, and returning vets in the growing and amorphous antiwar movement.

With each passing week Muhammad Ali, who four years earlier had sounded downright unpatriotic, sounded more like a prophet. As a result he was embraced by a generation of college students eager to hear what he had to say:

I had a ball, drivin' to the colleges and stayin' at the inns and meetin' the students, the black power groups, the white hippies, and we'd all have sessions on what we was gonna talk about and dinner was then planned in the hall, and we'd go to the student union buildin' and have the meetin' and they'd ask me questions, all the boys and girls, black and white. Like what should we do, or what do you think is gonna happen here, you know—just like I was one of those sleepy-lookin' Senators up in the capital.

Ali is no fool, and he knows talking to students is different from spouting badly rhymed verse to a gaggle of eager-beaver reporters for some good press. Standing at a podium and speaking to an auditorium filled with students requires homework:

Putting the lectures together was hard work. I had six of them, and first I wrote out all my ideas on paper. Then I wrote them out again on note cards, studied them every day, and practiced giving speeches in front of the mirror with [my wife] Belinda listening. Sometimes I tape recorded it so I could hear myself and learn how to improve what I said. I did that for about three months until I was ready, and the first speeches turned out good. Talking is whole lot easier than fighting. I must have gone to two hundred colleges, and I enjoyed the speaking. It made me happy.

They didn't love everything he had to say. His views on the war, his inability to fight for a living, the stripping of his title, and black pride were well received. His views on interracial dating, marijuana, the proper role of women, and homosexuality were not. And the audiences let him know it.

But one thing came across loud and clear: his caring, sincere, and straight talk.

"If He's Ready, I'm Ready"

By Keith Kincaid

"I'll believe I have a fight when I'm in the ring and I hear the bell," Ali admitted earlier this year.

Well, now he's heard two.

The first rang on October 26 when he faced Jerry Quarry in Atlanta (where there is no boxing commission and the mayor had the last word).

Ali last fought on March 22, 1967. Over three and half years ago.

Ali was twenty-five and just reaching his physical peak when a brilliant boxing career was cut short—not by a more skillful opponent, but by the dubious combination of state boxing commissions and the feds, neither of which wanted to allow him to fight in the face of his refusal to serve in Vietnam.

Time is a terrible thing, especially if you're an athlete.

In recent months, however, it became clear that the forces opposed to his ever fighting again (in the ring, that is) were being questioned and challenged, at precisely the same time that the government and the military's justification for the carnage called Vietnam was likewise being questioned and challenged.

Downtown Atlanta was turned into one big party for the fight. People from all over came to celebrate the return of the king. The night of the fight Atlanta looked more like Hollywood.

The chauffeur-driven cars rolled up to the hotel entrances one after another. The people who stepped out of the limos were all appropriately dressed and bejeweled. Nearly every black celebrity on the planet was present and accounted for.

The question was, could he come back?

There were cheers when he entered the ring—unlike when he left nearly four years ago. As much as anything it showed how much Americans had changed in their views on race and the war. Although some things remained the same. The ring announcer referred to him as Cassius Clay. Ali came out of his corner, arms held high. He did the Ali Shuffle—crisscrossing his legs back and forth with amazing speed. The SRO crowd erupted with wild cheering.

From the opening bell Ali had been longing to hear, the fighter looked like he had never been away. Quarry was strong but too slow; Ali's lightning combinations were landing consistently on Quarry's inviting face. In the middle of the third round a sharp right opened a deep cut over his left eye (a wound that would later require eleven stitches).

TKO, round three.

Such a short fight didn't convince spectators that Muhammad Ali could go the distance if pressed.

Last night, six weeks after the Quarry fight, Ali faced tough Argentine champ Oscar Bonavena at New York City's Madison Square Garden. Bonavena, a.k.a. Ringo, was a brawler, not a boxer. Ali didn't take him seriously and didn't train nearly as hard as he had for the Quarry fight.

Ali entered the ring wearing a red robe, white trunks, and white shoes with red tassels. The tassels moved about as little as he did. In the first round Ali looked heavy and dull. His punches didn't have the speed and accuracy that everyone had come to expect. He fought flat-footed for fourteen rounds.

In the fifteenth Ali finally caught Ringo, who appeared not to be paying attention at the time, and knocked him out.

But Bonavena isn't Smokin' Joe Frazier—considered by most non-Ali fans to be the current heavyweight champion. Asked after the Quarry fight about Joe, Ali said, "If he's ready, I'm ready."

As Muhammad Ali knows better than anyone, talk's cheap.

The Fight of the Century

By Keith Kincaid

"Bring on Frazier" was the only thing Muhammad Ali had to say when he learned he was getting back his license to box.

Tomorrow night he gets his wish. Like they say, be careful what you wish for.

As Salieri did with Mozart, Frazier blames Ali for his lack of popularity.

He's got a point.

The 1964 Olympic gold medal winner spent his entire pro career in the long shadow cast by Ali. A shadow that became even darker during Ali's years in exile—years that coincided with and eclipsed Frazier's official and semiofficial (it's a long story) reign as heavyweight champion of the non-Ali world.

Back then Ali, who was busy speaking to thousands of adoring college kids, showed some genuine R-E-S-P-E-C-T to Frazier, though: "I can't blame Joe Frazier for accepting the title under the conditions he did. . . . Joe's got four or five children to feed. He's worked in a meat-packing house all his life and deserves a break. He would have fought me if he had the chance. Joe Frazier wasn't just given the title. He had to fight for it, and he had to fight the best around except for me, so I can't take nothing from him. He had to keep on living, regardless of what happened to me."

Frazier has been training for the most important fight of his life in upstate New York, away from everyone. It suits him. He has trained even harder than usual, running six miles a day over rocky hills and boxing eight to ten rounds. James Brown may be the hardest-working man in show business, but Joe Frazier's the hardest-working man in the boxing business.

Ali has been training in Miami Beach, away from no one. It suits him. Each day there have been the usual crowds, who watched him go through his routine. In his usual not-so-serious way he took Frazier seriously, sort of, but he didn't train as hard as Frazier.

The now obligatory, derogatory prefight buildup was, as expected, regrettable.

Ali spouted the usual mix of insults and grammatically challenged, bad poetry:

> Joe's gonna come out smokin'
> But I ain't gonna be jokin'
> I'll be pickin' and pokin'
> Pouring water on his smokin'
> This might shock and amaze ya
> But I'm gonna destroy Joe Frazier.

But most of it didn't really seem to get to Joe (whose reported high blood pressure predates Ali); that is, until he called him "the gorilla."

Joe Frazier was not happy about being called that derogatory slur. And lots of other folks thought it was needlessly cruel as well.

Come what may tomorrow night at New York's sold-out-for-months, sure-to-be-packed-with-celebs Madison Square Garden, these two truly great undefeated heavyweights will settle it. And they'll settle for $2.5 million each—win, lose, or draw. The largest purse in boxing history. Another three hundred million people in thirty-six countries will be watching on closed-circuit TV.

The Frazier/Ali battle is indeed gearing up to be the fight of the century.

MADISON SQ GARDEN

New York City

Frazier Takes Title from Ali

Wins Unanimous Fifteen-Round Decision

Ali Floored in the Fifteenth

Muhammad Ali vs. Joe Frazier
The Fight of the Century

DATE: March 8, 1971
PLACE: Madison Square Garden, NYC

ROUND-BY-ROUND SCORECARD

ROUND	REFEREE	JUDGE #1	JUDGE #2
ONE	Ali	Ali	Frazier
TWO	Ali	Ali	Ali
THREE	Frazier	Frazier	Frazier
FOUR	Frazier	Frazier	Frazier
FIVE	Frazier	Frazier	Ali
SIX	Ali	Frazier	Frazier
SEVEN	Ali	Frazier	Frazier
EIGHT	Frazier	Frazier	Frazier
NINE	Ali	Ali	Ali
TEN	Ali	Ali	Frazier
ELEVEN	Frazier	Frazier	Frazier
TWELVE	Even	Frazier	Frazier
THIRTEEN	Frazier	Ali	Frazier
FOURTEEN	Frazier	Ali	Ali
FIFTEEN	Frazier	Frazier	Frazier

June 29, 1971

Ali KO's Supreme Court

8-0 Decision

Reverses 1967 Draft Conviction

Clears Champ of All Charges

Rules Religious Beliefs Sincere

January 23, 1973
Kingston, Jamaica

Foreman Batters Frazier for TKO Victory

Becomes Heavyweight Champion

Frazier Knocked Down Six Times

Ref Stops Fight in Second Round

SPORTSWORLD WEEKLY

Ken Who?

By Keith Kincaid

Last night Muhammad Ali came one step closer to reclaiming what he, and many boxing fans, feel is *his* title. A title currently held by George Foreman.

Six months ago Ali had taken a giant step backward.

He didn't think former marine Ken Norton had a chance in the world of beating him—even though he was ranked number seven. So he didn't bother to train hard for the fight. The night before he was, according to ABC-TV's Howard Cosell, laughing and joking at a party and then later entertaining people in the hotel coffee shop till dawn.

Ali came into the ring wearing a robe given to him by Elvis Presley in Las Vegas. It said PEOPLE'S CHOICE on the back. Ali weighed 221 pounds and looked flabby around the middle.

From the moment of the opening bell, Ali seemed sluggish. His punches had little power to them. In the second round Norton sent a crashing left to Ali's jaw—Ali never did like southpaws. He felt a sharp pain and could taste blood in his throat. When he went to his corner between rounds, he asked his cornermen how he could tell if his jaw was broken. He was told it would make a sound like two plates struck together. Ali tried it and could hear the sound. He refused to stop fighting, however, even though there were more than ten rounds to go. He felt he could still win. But it turned out that he couldn't.

Ken Norton, who dominated the twelfth and final round, was awarded a split decision (one judge and the ref gave the fight to Norton; the other judge disagreed). Joe Frazier jumped into the ring to hug Norton. By now the pain in Ali's face was almost more than he could stand. It was so painful he told his partner in crime, Cosell, he couldn't talk! Still, Ali coolly combed his hair and waved to his wife before he was whisked out of sight. That night he was sent to the hospital to have his jaw set.

The Norton fight was the last straw for many of Ali's remaining fans. Among them was Howard Cosell, who predicted Ali's career was over. The newspaper headlines the next day told the whole story: MUHAMMAD IS FINISHED; END OF AN ERA; BEATEN BY A NOBODY; BIG MOUTH SHUT FOR ALL TIME.

Ali headed for Louisville with his wife and their daughter Maryum. He needed to rest and to see the people who cared about him. He went to his aunt Coretta's for a family reunion. He spent long hours with his mother, father, and brother. He rested.

Six months later Muhammad Ali was ready for a return bout with Norton. This time he trained hard for the fight, and he shed nine pounds.

It was a close fight all the way. Norton was the more aggressive fighter as Ali danced away from danger. The crowd was divided: You could hear dueling "Ali" or "Norton" chants periodically. This time Ali won the split decision. But most felt that Norton had outfought Ali and had truly won the fight.

The question remains: Was the three-and-a-half-year layoff simply too much?

JANUARY 29, 1974

MADISON SQ GARDEN

New York City

Ali Beats Frazier in Rematch

TWELVE-ROUND UNANIMOUS DECISION

Nontitle Bout

ALI TO TAKE ON FOREMAN

Requiem for a Friendship

By Keith Kincaid

Once they were worthy opponents. Fierce adversaries, but friends nevertheless.

But that was long ago.

1967–1970: Ali's years in exile, when he lost his boxing license and, perhaps worse, his spot in the limelight. Although blue-collar Joe Frazier didn't agree with Ali's radical politics, he stood by him when most didn't. "Ain't right to take away a man's pick and shovel" was how Joe put it.

Frazier was considered the number one contender for the title unwillingly vacated by Ali. To help him out, Frazier agreed to stage public "confrontations" so Ali could remain in the public eye. Short memory and all that. Frazier even lent Ali money from time to time.

But once Ali beat Quarry, got his license back, and signed to fight Joe in New York City's Madison Square Garden on March 8, 1971, Ali changed his tune.

All signs of their friendship were gone, replaced by Ali's contempt as he incessantly and publicly ridiculed Joe, calling him "ugly" and "stupid." Frazier was the white man's champion, Ali pronounced. It was mean, personal, and racial, and Frazier felt betrayed. He took it hard and never forgot and never forgave.

The Fight of the Century was how it was billed, and it was.

For the first time in boxing history undefeated heavyweight champions faced each other. If Ali lost, he promised, he would crawl across the ring on his hands and knees and tell Joe Frazier *he* was the greatest.

Ali came out smokin', knowing it's best to get Smokin' Joe early because he only gets stronger and more insistent as the fight goes on.

Of course there was time for clowning—Ali shaking his head and telling the crowd, "No, I ain't hurt," when Frazier landed a punch (but Frazier knew better), and talking from time to time even though the ref kept warning him to stop.

Meanwhile, workmanlike Joe Frazier, with his patented, piston-driven, purposely nonrhythmic head-bobbing relentlessness, kept coming and landing.

By the fifth Ali had taken more solid shots than he'd taken in his entire pro career. And Frazier, gaining confidence by the round, waved him to come on in and get some more.

In the ninth Ali was staggered by a lethal left hook; his legs buckled and his eyes glazed, but he wouldn't go down. Pride was all that kept him up, but it was enough. Instinctively he exaggerated just how wobbly he was— cartoon wobbly. Or was he exaggerating? For a moment Joe had to stop and consider: *Did I hurt him enough to go in for the kill?*

The fight was razor close when Frazier floored Ali with a vicious left to the jaw in the fifteenth. Ali, miraculously, got up at the count of three. Most fighters would have called it a night. Pride again.

But the fight was Frazier's fair and square. Unanimous decision.

It was Muhammad Ali's first loss as a professional fighter.

But in the immediate aftermath of the fight Ali began to publicly deny that he'd lost. Only white people thought he'd lost, Ali explained. Privately, however, he admitted that he had underestimated the devastating power of Frazier's left hook.

When a reporter told Ali that Frazier said he probably wouldn't want to fight him again, Ali shot back: "Oh, how wrong he is."

Which is how we got to Ali/Frazier II.

Frazier had lost the crown to George Foreman a year earlier, so Ali/Frazier II wasn't a title match. Still, there was plenty at stake: The winner earned the right to have a shot at Foreman and the title.

But that wasn't all that was at stake.

Since their first fight the two had come to truly and deeply dislike each other. What had begun as a professional rivalry had become a mutual, personal vendetta.

Five days before the fight both fighters appeared on Howard Cosell's *Wide World of Sports* TV show. Their epic March 1971 fight was going to be shown on home TV for the first time, and they were providing the commentary. It didn't take long for the atmosphere to become heated.

Frazier said something about Ali's going to the hospital after the fight—a guaranteed hot button given Ali's vanity and desire to hide how much hard work, pain, and suffering goes into his craft.

Ali, visibly annoyed, asked: "Why'd you say that about the hospital, Joe? Why'd you even bring that up the hospital. I wasn't going to talk about the hospital. Everybody knows I went to the hospital for ten minutes. You were in the hospital for three weeks. You're ignorant, Joe."

Within seconds Frazier was up and standing in front of Ali, Rahman Ali (who had been needling Frazier from off stage) joined in, and Ali and Frazier were grappling on the studio floor.

On January 28, 1974, the curtain opened on act two.

Ali was all business this time: no clowning, no talking. Just counterpunching, piling up the points, moving silkily away from the trouble his laser eyes could invariably spot just in time, and slipping most of Frazier's punches. Calling on all his boxing skill, ring sense, and experience, Ali won a unanimous decision.

Unanimous as far as the judges and the ref were concerned. Some sportswriters and fans felt Ali was given a gift—that the fight was a draw, or even that Frazier had won.

Frazier wants one more chance, and Ali is willing to oblige: "I'm not going to duck Joe, I'm going to give him all the chances he wants."

Joe Frazier will have to wait in line, though.

First comes George Foreman.

"Peace with Honor"

At noon on August 9, 1974, Richard Nixon, hounded by the Watergate investigation and the threat of impeachment, became the first American president to resign.

During his six years in office he widened the war in Vietnam, intensified the bombing, and increased the death toll on both sides. Finally, in January 1973, a peace agreement was signed, and subsequently all American ground troops were withdrawn from Vietnam.

"Peace with honor" had been, according to Nixon, achieved.

After waving good-bye to his staff, Nixon departed for his home in San Clemente, California.

Ali and Belinda

Muhammad Ali is seen here in late August 1974, seven months after defeating Joe Frazier and two months before winning back the heavyweight title from George Foreman in the Rumble in the Jungle.

He and his wife, Belinda, are outside their Cherry Hill, New Jersey, apartment building. While Belinda readies her camera, Ali looks off into the distance and fantasizes about the mansion he's going to build someday.

A week from today—at 4 a.m. on October 30, 1974, to be precise—the much-anticipated heavyweight championship bout between the current title holder, George Foreman, and Muhammad Ali will get under way in Kinshasa, Zaire. The fight is taking place in Africa thanks to the efforts of the promoter and the willingness of Zaire's president to guarantee the boxers that they will split a $10 million purse.

On January 22, 1973, Foreman knocked Joe Frazier to the canvas six times in two rounds, winning on a TKO and taking the championship from Frazier. Almost exactly a year later Ali defeated Frazier, after losing their first fight. The thirty-two-year-old Ali is attempting to become only the second boxer in history (Patterson was the first) to regain the title.

As we did back in '64 for Liston vs. Clay, we asked some of our town's most knowledgeable boxing fans:

WHO DO YOU THINK WILL WIN THE UPCOMING RUMBLE IN THE JUNGLE: MUHAMMAD ALI OR GEORGE FOREMAN?

Here are the best responses:

I think it's going to be a draw, and I'll tell you why: They're very evenly matched.

Both men won Olympic gold medals when they were young—Ali in '60 and Foreman in '68.

Both are big—although at six feet four inches, Foreman might have an inch on Ali. But that's all. Everyone thinks Foreman's a monster—it's the same thing they thought about Liston back in the day. That is, until the two of them came face-to-face in the center of the ring for the first round of the first fight. People were stunned to see Ali, although he was Cassius then, staring *down* at Liston. As a matter of fact, Ali's not only bigger than Liston, he's bigger than Dempsey and Louis. And of course Foreman is one of the biggest heavyweights ever—just watch film of the two Frazier fights; Foreman towers over him.

So like I say, they're evenly matched. Both big. Both formidable.

It's going to be razor close, if you ask me.

Foreman's simply invincible. No contest.

First of all, Foreman's record is 41–0 with thirty-seven KOs. In fact, he has the highest KO percentage in boxing history. Now there's a stat for you. Not one of his last eight fights went past the second round!

Second, Foreman's a lot younger than Clay—seven years, if I remember correctly. And that three-and-a-half-year layoff for draft dodging didn't do him any good, I'll tell you that.

I'd say the fight won't last more than three rounds.

TKO, Foreman, in the third—fourth, maybe. Tops.

I believe Ken Norton beat Ali in the first fight when he broke Ali's jaw. And he gave him trouble in the second fight.

Foreman knocked Norton out—and it only took him two rounds.

Ali's two fights against Joe Frazier went the distance, and Ali lost the first one and just squeaked by in the second.

Foreman knocked Frazier down six times in two rounds when he dethroned him. He hit him so hard he actually lifted Smokin' Joe clear off the ground.

Foreman beat Norton. Foreman beat Frazier. Foreman will beat Ali.

Foreman by a knockout. Ask me a hard question.

I teach high school athletics and coach varsity football here in Edina. And let me tell you something—it's all about how you train.

Now, this three-and-a-half-year layoff concerns me. Ali has gotten out of the habit of training every day. And I mean every day. It's hard to get back in the saddle, I can tell you that.

Now I hear he's back to training seriously for this fight. Working with sparring partners on his weaknesses, having them hit him with body shots to toughen up his stomach muscles; and once he got to Africa, sparring earlier and earlier each day to get used to fighting at four a.m. I also hear he's eating a healthy diet again—no more ice cream and malted, which is what did him in against Norton—veal, fish, no beef, and drinking only distilled water and juice.

If Ali comes into that ring in peak condition—and I suspect he will—then it's his fight.

Foreman beat Jose Roman, who was the heavyweight champion of Puerto Rico. He knocked him out in fifty seconds. Fastest championship fight in history.
C'mon. Ali doesn't stand a chance.

Foreman.
I mean, why go against the bookies in Las Vegas? They spend all day figuring out how to make money betting on sporting events, and they have him winning, with the odds four to one. You think they don't know what's going on?
You think they don't have the inside scoop?
Believe me, they do.

Ali.
Intelligence counts. Ali has it, Foreman doesn't.
It's as simple as that.
Watch.

The losers will be the people of Zaire and anyone else who believes that these two jokers are fighting in Africa for any reason other than money. Do you know that the five million each of these guys is getting is more than Dempsey and Marciano made in their lifetime? What a crime. Even Ali's manager, Herbert Muhammad, admits that his man would fight anywhere the money is.

October 30, 1974
Kinshasa, Zaire

RUMBLE IN THE JUNGLE

Ali, #32, Regains Heavyweight Title

Only Second Boxer in History to Recapture Crown

Employs "Rope-a-Dope" Strategy

KO's Foreman with Powerful
Combination in Round Eight

"Who's Your Hero?"
CONTEST

Earlier this year the History Teachers of America, through our ad hoc Committee to Stem the Rising Tide of Historical Amnesia, launched its first annual (hopefully) "Who's Your Hero?" Contest.

The question posed was: Who in American life—past or present—is your hero and why?

The answer could be in any form: essay, biography, memoir, short story, poem, play, song, drawing, painting, etc. The contest was open to all students.

The deadline for entries was December 12, 1974, and we received over ten thousand responses! Most of the subjects chosen were familiar ones: John F. Kennedy, Martin Luther King Jr., Jackie Robinson, Charles Lindbergh. But there were many surprises: John Brown, Bobby Fischer, Cesar Chavez, Malcolm X, and Amelia Earhart, to name just a few.

Our panel of five distinguished (and underpaid) teacher/judges reviewed each and every submission, narrowed the ten thousand down to five hundred, then a hundred, and finally the top three winners.

Third place was awarded to students from Cliffside Park Junior High School in San Francisco who wrote a narrative poem about Helen Keller and Anne Sullivan. Students from Somerville Junior High School in Massachusetts took second place with a play about Rosa Parks and the Montgomery bus boycott.

The winning submission was from Mrs. Klinger's history class at John Jay Middle School in Katonah, New York. Their subject: Muhammad Ali and his comeback in the Rumble in the Jungle. Their entry was in the form of pencil drawings and captions of that now-famous fight.

Their accompanying statement read:

Muhammad Ali personifies many characteristics we admire: courage, honesty, sincerity, and integrity. His actions, under adverse conditions and circumstances, have shown us that these are not just words you memorize in school but ones that can be applied in the real world.

He has always spoken the truth as he sees it and has stood behind his principles—regardless of the consequences.

When he refused to be inducted into the military and voiced his opposition to the war in Vietnam, our so-called leaders were busy misleading us, and the antiwar movement had not yet become a force to be reckoned with.

We all have friends or family, or know someone who has friends or family, who have returned from Vietnam physically or psychologically damaged. And some of us were close to boys who did not return at all.

Muhammad Ali paid a price for his radical political views: His title was taken away from him, and his license to box was revoked at the very time he was reaching his prime. This cost him not only millions of dollars he would have made inside the ring, but millions more he could have made in endorsements. But he never flinched.

When the Supreme Court of the United States admitted that he had been unjustly punished, Ali spoke no words of bitterness or blame—further testament to his character.

Although he could not reclaim those lost years, he could reclaim his lost title. We were too young to have witnessed his boxing exploits back in the sixties, but we have fathers, older brothers, and uncles who have made them come alive for us. With them we watched Ali as he began his arduous journey on the comeback trail: past pretenders and contenders till he finally defeated a bona fide dangerous foe in Joe Frazier.

Ali earned the right to face the heavyweight champion of the world, George Foreman, in Zaire.

The oddsmakers and experts said he didn't stand a chance. He was too old. Past his prime. Foreman was too big. Too powerful.

All of this was just fuel for Ali's fire.

When Muhammad Ali miraculously prevailed over Foreman in the Rumble in the Jungle (to become only the second man in history to reclaim the heavyweight title), it was a victory for underdogs everywhere.

The way he did it—by calling on his years of experience and know-how, by training perhaps harder than he ever had for a fight, by knowing his opponent's flaws and figuring out how to capitalize on them, by fighting a smart fight from the opening bell, and most importantly by having a transcendental belief in his own abilities—was awesome.

Muhammad Ali's life challenges us to think for ourselves, question conventional wisdom, discover what we truly believe in and what we are willing to risk on behalf of that belief, and consider what our proper role is in American society. His life also teaches us that to do any of these things, you first have to believe in yourself.

The dictionary tells us a hero is someone who performs brave deeds and has noble qualities. But we think there's more. We think a hero is someone who inspires others to elevate their game.

That's why Muhammad Ali is our hero.

Sincerely,

Lisa Abrams

Morgan Schaus

Sidney Schaus

Julia Smith

Mary Hudson

Peter Smith

Catherine Troiano

Lauren Ford

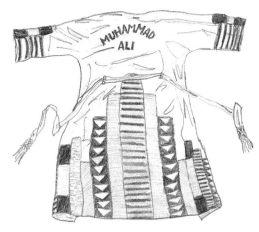

This is the wool and satin African robe that Muhammad Ali wore when he entered the ring to fight George Foreman.—Lisa Abrams, 14

The flags of the United States and Zaire are displayed as the national anthems of both countries are played.—Morgan Schaus, 13

Muhammad Ali and George Foreman stand face-to-face before the opening bell. Ali is saying something not nice to Foreman.—Julia Smith, 13

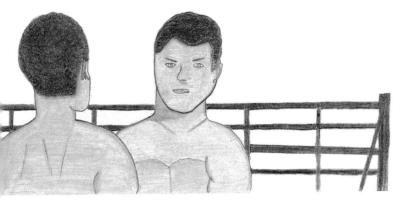

Muhammad Ali is taunting Foreman from his corner at the start of the seventh round.—Catherine Troiano, 14

Round one. Ali throws a right hand that lands hard on Foreman's head.—Mary Hudson, 13

George Foreman is being counted out after he was knocked down by Ali with only seconds to go in the eighth round.—Lauren Ford, 14

Ali is leaning back on the ropes in the "rope-a-dope," a tactic he invented and will use throughout the fight.—Peter Smith, 14

Ali has Foreman backed agaist the ropes.
—Sidney Schaus, 13

MAN-ON-THE-STREET

AUDACITY.

GOING AGAINST THE RULES LIKE HE DID—IN AND OUT OF THE RING—HIS WHOLE LIFE.

I MEAN, HE COMES OUT IN THE FIRST ROUND AND HITS FOREMAN SMACK IN THE FACE WITH A STRAIGHT RIGHT. NOW, IF YOU KNOW ANYTHING ABOUT BOXING, WHICH THANKS TO TWO OLDER BROTHERS I DO, YOU KNOW THAT YOU'RE NOT SUPPOSED TO LEAD WITH A RIGHT. ANYWAY, IT JUST TAKES TOO LONG TO GET ACROSS YOUR BODY, ACROSS YOUR CHEST AND LAND. TAKES WAY TOO MUCH TIME. THAT'S WHY EVERYONE, INCLUDING ALI, JABS, JABS, JABS.

ANYWAY, WHERE WAS I? OH, RIGHT, ROUND ONE. SO ALI PUNCHES FOREMAN RIGHT IN THE GRILL WITH THIS TOTALLY UNORTHODOX STRAIGHT RIGHT. LIKE TO SAY, *HERE, FOOL, TAKE THAT.* IT'S INSULTING THAT ALI IS EVEN ATTEMPTING IT AND MORE INSULTING THAT HE'S GETTING AWAY WITH IT. YOU CAN SEE THE LOOK ON FOREMAN'S FACE. AT FIRST HE'S SO ANGRY HE CAN SPIT. BUT THEN HE'S CONFUSED, WHICH ISN'T GOOD. 'CAUSE THEN HE'S ANGRY, INSULTED, AND CONFUSED ALL AT THE SAME TIME, AND THAT'S TOO MANY THINGS FOR ANY FIGHTER TO THINK ABOUT IN THE MIDDLE OF THE RING. ESPECIALLY A FIGHTER LIKE FOREMAN, WHO HAS TROUBLE THINKING ABOUT ONE THING AT A TIME.

THE FIGHT WAS OVER AFTER THE FIRST ROUND. AFTER THOSE FIRST TWO STRAIGHT RIGHTS.

FOREMAN NEVER RECOVERED AND HE NEVER STOOD A CHANCE AGAINST THE RINGMASTER AFTER THAT.

ALI'S A TRICKSTER, AND HE TRICKED GEORGE FOREMAN REAL GOOD. TALKING BEFORE THE FIGHT ABOUT HOW HE WAS GOING TO BE DANCIN' AND DOIN' THE ALI SHUFFLE, SO THAT FOREMAN'S HANDLERS IMMEDIATELY WENT TO WORK DEVELOPING A STRATEGY TO COUNTER A STRATEGY THAT ALI NEVER INTENDED TO USE. HE JUST WANTED FOREMAN TO WASTE HIS TIME PREPARING FOR IT, KNOWING THAT POOR, PLODDING GEORGE WOULD NEVER BE ABLE TO THINK ON HIS FEET AND IMPROVISE WHEN ALI CAME OUT FROM THE GET-GO WITH A COMPLETELY DIFFERENT STRATEGY.

ANGELO DUNDEE WON THE FIGHT, JUST LIKE HE WON THE FIRST LISTON FIGHT WHEN HE MADE ALI GO OUT FOR ROUND FIVE, OR WHATEVER IT WAS, EVEN THOUGH CLAY—YOU REMEMBER THAT NAME, DON'T YOU?—HAD SOME SUBSTANCE IN HIS EYES AND COULDN'T SEE WORTH A DAMN.

WELL, THIS TIME DUNDEE HAD PEOPLE SPYING ON FOREMAN WHILE HE TRAINED IN ZAIRE. AND DUNDEE ALSO WORKED HIS MAGIC COMING TO THE STADIUM HOURS BEFORE THE FIGHT AND PUTTING SOME RESIN ON THE RING FLOOR TO MAKE SURE IT WAS FAST FOR HIS BOY, AND THEN LOOSENING THE TOP ROPE SO ALI COULD UNVEIL THEIR SECRET "ROPE-A-DOPE" PLAN AND LEAN BACK SO FAR ON THAT TOP ROPE, SO FAR OVER THE FIRST ROW, THAT HE LOOKED LIKE HE WAS CHECKING FOR RAIN. THAT WAY HE COULD KEEP HIS PRETTY-BOY FACE OUT OF GEORGE'S RANGE; CRUISE FOR PART OF A ROUND, CONSERVING ENERGY; AND LET GEORGE EXHAUST HIMSELF AND GET ARM WEARY PUNCHING THE HELL OUT OF ALI'S ROCK-HARD TORSO.

A BIG REASON WAS THE SIXTY-THREE THOUSAND PEOPLE IN THE STADIUM ALL CHANTING "ALI, BOMA YE," WHICH, ROUGHLY TRANSLATED, MEANS "ALI, KILL HIM."

CHRIST, IT WAS LIKE ALI HAD THE HOME ICE ADVANTAGE AND FOREMAN WAS PLAYING AN AWAY GAME. A WAY AWAY GAME. BETWEEN ROUNDS ALI WOULD WAVE HIS ARMS UP AND DOWN, EGGING THEM ON—NOT THAT THEY NEEDED IT.

CAN YOU IMAGINE HOW DEMORALIZING IT MUST HAVE BEEN FOR POOR GEORGE?

DID YOU SEE HIM WHEN HE LEFT THE RING, STILL DAZED AND WEARING, LIKE, A GREEN TOWEL OVER HIS SHOULDER? NOT THE RED ROBE SAYING "HEAVYWEIGHT CHAMPION OF THE WORLD," LIKE HE DID WHEN HE ENTERED?

THERE WAS HARDLY ANYONE WITH HIM. HE TOOK THAT LONG WALK PRACTICALLY ALONE.

LONESOME GEORGE.

I THINK IT WAS JUST TOO EARLY IN THE MORNING FOR GEORGE. HE LIKES TO SLEEP IN. FIGHTING AT DAWN JUST AIN'T HIS STYLE. PLUS, EVEN THOUGH HE WAS BORN AND RAISED IN TEXAS, THE EIGHTY-SIX-DEGREE HEAT DIDN'T HELP.

ALI'S SUPERIOR TRAINING AND CONDITIONING WON THE FIGHT. IT WAS OBVIOUS DURING THE MIDDLE ROUNDS, WHEN HE LAY BACK ON THE ROPES AND LET FOREMAN WHALE AWAY ON HIS BODY, WHICH HE HAD WORKED ON MAKING ROCK HARD. I CAN'T IMAGINE HOW MANY SIT-UPS HE DID EVERY DAY TO GET READY TO TAKE THAT KIND OF PUNISHMENT.

FOREMAN LOST THE FIGHT, ALI DIDN'T WIN IT. FOREMAN FOUGHT STUPID—HE WAS LOST AND UNABLE TO CHANGE TACTICS MIDSTREAM.

IT WAS JUST LIKE ALI SAID BEFORE THE FIGHT. FOREMAN LOOKED LIKE A MUMMY COMING OFF HIS STOOL AT THE SOUND OF THE BELL—STRIDING STIFF-LEGGED ACROSS THE RING RIGHT AT ALI—AND THINKING ONLY ONE THING: I'M GONNA KNOCK THIS GUY OUT WITH ONE PUNCH.

OF COURSE, THE ONE PUNCH NEVER HAPPENED.

Saigon

On the morning of April 29, 1975, North Vietnamese troops were about to take over Saigon, the capital of South Vietnam. The overly optimistic American ambassador (who thought there was still time for a negotiated peace) ordered an evacuation only at the very last minute, resulting in chaos, panic, and, at times, hysteria.

Americans and their dependents, as well as the Vietnamese who worked for them (and were therefore considered "at risk" if left behind) and their families, were to be taken by helicopters to U.S. aircraft carriers deployed offshore.

This helicopter—one of seventy that shuttled evacuees to the carriers—is situated on the rooftop of an embassy building. A CIA operative is helping people up the ladder and onto the helicopter.

The Thrilla in Manila

By Keith Kincaid

It will be a killer
And a chiller
And a thrilla
When I get the gorilla
In Manila.

Everyone knew who the gorilla was.

Ali took to carrying a black rubber gorilla in his pocket and would whip it out at any and every opportunity so he could punch it just like he would Joe Frazier. Even Ali loyalists thought he had crossed a line.

Frazier, of course, had other plans: "Well, I guess he's gonna talk. Ain't no way to stop him, but there'll come that moment when he's gonna hear that knock on the door, gonna hear it's time to go to the ring, and then he's gonna remember what it's like to be in with me, how hard and long that night's gonna be."

President Ferdinand Marcos had put up millions to have the fight staged at the Philippine capital. The president and his wife treated Ali like he was visiting royalty; as always, the champ fully enjoyed his celeb status. Adoring crowds followed him everywhere. Frazier arrived to no fanfare and was largely ignored. Presumably he's used to that. We didn't say happy, just used to it. He passed the time quietly in the Spartan solitude of his hotel suite, playing cards with his sparring partners.

Ali/Frazier has become the most bitter rivalry in all of sports history.

Their once-amicable relationship has devolved into a blood feud. And no one doubted that, once inside that ring, they would try to hurt each other as badly as possible, knowing it was the only way to come out on top.

Or at all.

This, their third meeting, was expected to settle once and for all who was the best. The loser would most likely be forced to hang up the gloves.

Ali came in a 2–1 favorite and reportedly got an estimated $6 million; Frazier got half of that. An estimated seven hundred million people in sixty-four countries were watching on closed-circuit TV via the first worldwide satellite transmission of a heavyweight bout.

To ensure a prime-time American viewing audience, the fight began at 10:45 a.m.

Ali opened fast, hoping to put Frazier away early, hitting him with an assortment of clean, stinging shots to the head. They were doing damage but not slowing Smokin' Joe down—he only smiled when hit, his mouthpiece accentuating the gesture until he resembled a demented jack-o'-lantern. Taking advantage of his extraordinary reach—unusually long even for someone his size and only more so against someone as short as Frazier—Ali held his left arm straight out, like the big kid in the school yard taunting one of the smaller boys. Frazier just batted it aside and kept on coming.

At the sound of the bell ending the second round Frazier, walking briskly to his corner, gave Ali a dismissive wave, as if to say, *What else can you show me?*

Over the next three rounds Ali modified his style, backing himself into the corners and letting Frazier have at it, much like he did in Zaire. When Frazier would back off a step or two, Ali, keeping his arms upraised, would wave him back in and Frazier would resume his relentless attack.

Periodically Ali, while still in the corner, would explode unexpectedly with a series of lightning-fast combinations. Still, Ali was taking some serious blows to the body from Frazier.

It was as if they had met privately before the fight and agreed that Ali would take the head, Frazier the body.

By the fifth round Frazier was getting stronger, gaining confidence, and starting to dominate the fight—although he was no longer smiling. His powerful body shots were starting to break through Ali's upraised and protective arms and find their targets: the kidney, liver, and heart areas; the places where pain resides.

In the sixth they exchanged vicious blows, and Frazier nailed Ali with two crushing lefts to the head—shots that would have sent most men to the canvas. But Muhammad Ali was not most men. He was, however, starting to look tired.

Throughout the fight both men broke clean when the bell sounded ending a round, and marched back to their respective corners. In the early rounds this seemed to show the discipline and professionalism of both men. Now, however, it looked more like they were both glad to leave the fury at the center of the ring for a momentary respite.

The fight looked even by the tenth, which may be why Ali changed tactics yet again and began to fight flat-footed—looking to get more power into his punches. And looking to knock Frazier out.

In the next round Ali was up on his toes, dancing and moving, but still Frazier was able to connect. In the twelfth Ali's quick hands enabled him to land a withering combination to Frazier's head, and he began to bleed from the mouth. Both eyes were now puffy, especially the left. It was possible Frazier could not see the right coming. For the first time he looked tired, and his punches had lost the power they had in the early and middle rounds. And no one knew that better than Ali.

Reaching down into some hidden reservoir of energy, Ali began the thirteenth again up on his toes and moving like the Ali of old. Midway through the round he hit Frazier so hard Joe's mouthpiece went flying several rows back into the crowd. Ali followed that up with repeated shots to the head. The crowd, sensing he was moving in for the kill, began to chant the familiar "Ali! Ali!"

But Joe Frazier would not go down.

It was a big round for Ali, and it came at a time when the fight was too close to call. Ali's face was completely drained of any emotions other than pain and exhaustion. Frazier now had a cut under his left eye, and both eyes were nearly closed—slits, really.

Muhammad Ali had taken the fight back from Joe Frazier.

Miraculously, Ali came out for the fourteenth still up on his toes, still moving, and hit Frazier, it seemed, at will with hard combinations. Sensing Frazier was near collapse, he kept up the savage punishment, throwing maybe as many as thirty straight punches.

But Frazier, though too weak to retaliate, would not fall.

At the end of the fourteenth Ali tried to walk strong to his corner, but there was a slight unsteadiness, like he himself wasn't sure if he was going to make it all the way there. For the first time in his career he slouched on his stool—he didn't sit or, as he sometimes does between rounds just to show he can, stand. He looked like he was literally going to cave in on himself, and his face was without expression. A void.

Ali told Dundee to cut the gloves off, that he was finished. Like he did eleven years earlier in the first Liston fight, his trainer ignored him, and continued preparing him to go back out for the last round.

Over in Frazier's corner Eddie Futch and the others were hovering over their fighter. The doctor came over to have a look, but Futch had already decided he wasn't going to let Frazier go out for the fifteenth round. Joe objected, but Futch wasn't hearing any of it. He'd been around too long, seen too many fighters suffer permanent damage—and worse.

"Sit down, son. It's over," he said to Frazier. "No one will forget what you did here today."

Futch notified the ref, who told Angelo Dundee.

Ali didn't even have the strength to look elated when he heard that he had won. He could barely stand and put his arms weakly up in the air. It was hard to tell if he was celebrating his victory or merely the fact that it was finally over. Then he collapsed onto the canvas.

After the fight he talked about retiring: "You may have seen the last of Ali. I want to get out of it. . . . What you saw tonight was next to death."

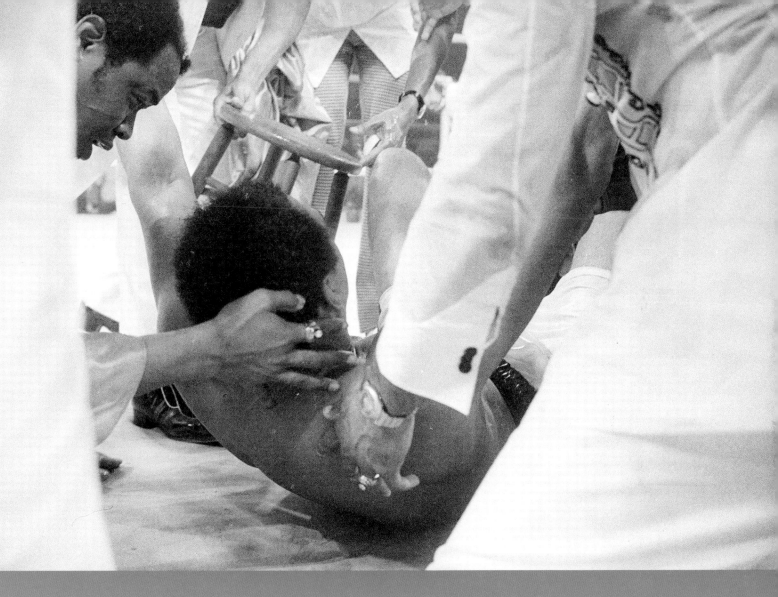

The Thrilla in Manila

By the time of their third fight—on October 1, 1975—Ali/Frazier had become the most bitter rivalry in sports history. The first two bouts were hard fought and razor close, ending in a unanimous decision for each.

In Manila, their most brutal battle yet, Frazier's longtime trainer, fearing permanent injury, would not let his fighter go out for the fifteenth (and final) round. A thoroughly exhausted Muhammad Ali, after hearing that he had won, collapsed onto the canvas.

February 16, 1978
Las Vegas, Nevada

24-Year-Old Unknown Leon Spinks Upsets Ali, 36

Wins Heavyweight Title

Fifteen-Round Split Decision

September 16, 1978
New Orleans, Louisiana

Ali Wins

Defeats Spinks in Fifteen Rounds

Unanimous Decision

Only Boxer in History to Regain Title Three Times

After Two-Year Retirement, Ali Will Return to the Ring

"Four-Time Champion, How Does That Sound?"

$8 Million Payday for Former Champ

Ali to Fight One-Time Sparring Partner Larry Holmes

Holmes Says:
"Ali Is Thirty-Eight Years Old. His Mind Is Making a Date That His Body Can't Keep."

Ali's Mother Speaks Out Publicly for the First Time:
"I Don't Want to See Him Fighting Anymore."

October 3, 1980

Las Vegas, Nevada

Larry Holmes Humiliates Former Champ

Ali Lands Less Than Ten Punches

Fails to Come out for Eleventh Round

December 12, 1981

Ali Loses Final Fight

Unanimous Ten-Round Decision vs. Berbick

"I'll Never Fight Again," Ali says.

Full Circle

By Keith Kincaid

There wasn't a dry eye in the house.

It was after midnight, and the opening ceremonies of the 1996 Summer Games in Atlanta were about to conclude with the lighting of the Olympic flame.

Swimmer Janet Evans ran the torch up the ramp. Traditionally, an athlete from the host country does the honors, so choosing the four-time gold medal winner made sense. At the top of the ramp Evans turned toward the huge crowd (and, not coincidentally, the TV cameras) and lifted the torch.

Then, suddenly materializing, or so it seemed, out of the shadows on the platform at the far end—just like in one of those cheesy magic acts he insists on performing at the drop of a rabbit in a hat—was the most famous athlete in history: fifty-four-year-old Muhammad Ali. In his right hand he held an unlit torch. Evans lit the torch with hers, and then Ali lifted it so all could see. His head and left hand shook from the Parkinson's syndrome he now lives with. Holding the torch securely with both hands, Ali then lit the cauldron that started the flame.

He was, of course, the perfect choice to light the Olympic flame. The eighty-five thousand present roared their approval as billions watched around the globe. No one had guessed Ali would be given the honor of lighting the torch—it was a well-kept secret (only those connected with the broadcast were informed). Even President Bill Clinton didn't know. He embraced Ali afterward, saying: "They didn't tell me who would light the flame, but when I saw it was you, I cried."

It had been more than a decade since he announced he had Parkinson's syndrome. Of course, many of us who had watched him closely and incessantly over the years saw the signs. The face that had once been constantly animated was now expressionless; like a mask. The man who had invented trash talk and rap now had slurred speech. Once he had had the fastest hands and feet in the history of the sport. But now his hands trembled beyond his control and his pace was slowed.

No longer could he float like a butterfly or sting like a bee.

Seeing him, this sportswriter found his thoughts drifting back to 1960, when I first began to cover him. We were both young and just starting out. Both looking for glory.

Back then, I mentioned in an article his brief part in a very good fight movie—more than that, really—*Requiem for a Heavyweight*. In it he plays a brash, young up-and-coming boxer—exactly what he was at the time (with the emphasis on "brash"). He is going against an aging fighter who was once also a contender but is no more. Having taken one punch too many, he is warned that the next one could cause permanent damage. Talk about irony.

Over the next thirty-plus years, I watched the boy become a man and charted every step as his career blossomed. I was ringside at all but a handful of his sixty-one professional fights. That was easy. That was fun. What was *not* fun was spending weeks on end in some godforsaken place like Zaire or Manila (you don't know what hot is till you've been to Manila) and jotting down Ali's every utterance in time for the afternoon edition. What was *not* fun was attending all those press conferences whose only purpose was to publicize the fight and were always about next to nothing. Or the prefight weigh-ins. Do you really have to make sure a heavyweight hasn't suddenly become a middleweight—and if you do, does everyone in the press (and their pals) have to attend? These prefight weigh-ins were about as necessary as your appendix (and could be the cause of a like amount of trouble). And how about those postfight postmortems, where everyone who could said "I told you so" and everyone who hadn't guessed the outcome correctly made up lame excuses for their error.

Except for Ali. He never did that. Well, almost never. He pretty much always owned up.

Back then, I wrote that he was a riddle wrapped in a mystery inside an enigma.

You would think after all this time I would have a pretty good handle on the guy. Be able to tell the real person from the one who hid behind all those masks he liked to wear: the childish clown; the outrageous, narcissistic pretty boy; the cruel, insensitive bully; the white-hating racist; the black Muslim destined to lead his people to the promised land; the happily married man who loved kids; the devout religious figure; and the PR man's dream come true.

Fact was I didn't. I didn't have a handle on the guy.

I think in simple terms. I'm a sportswriter. Win or lose. Make the shot or miss. Good guy or bad guy.

So which was he—a good guy or a bad guy?

I honestly couldn't have told you until ten years ago—which, if you think about it, is twenty-six years after I started covering him. Enough time.

In 1986 I wrote a story that settled it for me once and for all. It was titled "A Friend in Deed." Of course the story never made it into print. Stories like that never do.

It was about Ken Norton, a decent guy and more than a decent fighter. In case you forgot, both are a dime a dozen today.

Ken's main chance had come thirteen years earlier, in 1973. Ali was back from his three and a half years of forced exile from the sport he had all but redefined, courtesy of the U.S. government. He'd won twelve fights on the comeback trail—eight by KOs. But he'd lost the big one, the Fight of the Century, to Smokin' Joe. But Ali was undaunted. He was still on the hunt and was looking to take Joe on again, and to take on all comers along the way.

Norton, with his awkward southpaw style (the champ had trouble with southpaws), was a comer, maybe.

Truth is, Ken Norton thought it was an honor just to be in the same ring with Ali. That's not a good way to go into a fight, trust me. But Norton was smart and, even more relevant, a marine, and marines don't back down.

So what happened is Ken Norton, the nobody, who didn't really stand a chance, broke the champ's jaw and won a well-earned twelve-round unanimous decision. Upset doesn't come close to describing it.

Fast-forward to 1986. The champ was five years into his retirement and focusing on his new formidable foe, Parkinson's syndrome. But he was still one of the most famous—if not *the* most famous—faces on the planet. And Ken Norton—although he'd had a good run, spoiled only by key losses to George Foreman and Larry Holmes, which was nothing to be ashamed of there—was now just a footnote in boxing history thanks to his long-ago victory over the champ.

Norton was in a terrible car accident that year—1986. He was unconscious for quite a while, and when he wasn't, he had no memory of what had happened. His right side was partially paralyzed and his skull was fractured. The doctors advised him he might never walk again—or even talk (ironically, his jaw was broken). This was a diagnosis the positive-thinking Norton refused to accept. He was in the hospital for months, and for a time he was on the brink of the abyss we call depression.

Then one day there was Ali, at the hospital.

No sportswriters. No photographers. No TV cameras. No fight to promote and nothing to sell.

There he was at the foot of Norton's hospital bed, doing magic tricks with cards, making a handkerchief disappear, and levitating himself.

Just to help an old friend pass the time while he recuperated.

Like I said, the story never made it into print. But it's always stayed with me.

Only a handful of people knew, and I was honored to be one of them.

That's when I knew. Knew that Ali was a good guy after all.

But even if I was now satisfied that personally he was a good guy, what about politically?

Here I was wading in high muddy waters.

For those times, now known with misleading brevity (brevity being the enemy of truth, according to a wise man I read from time to time) as the sixties—which, by the way, didn't really end until the midseventies, but that's another story—were filled to overflowing with the drama and tragedy of the civil rights movement.

Of Rosa Parks; Martin Luther King Jr.; Diane Nash and John Lewis; Goodman, Schwerner, and Chaney; and Stokely Carmichael. Of the bus boycotts, sit-ins, Freedom Summer and Freedom Riders, and the endless marches. Of the southern towns that became permanently etched into the American consciousness: Oxford, Little Rock, Birmingham, Selma.

Of the assassinations, from Medgar Evars and Malcolm X to Martin Luther King Jr. and the Kennedy brothers.

And of the war that was never declared and never seemed to end. Of Robert McNamara, Rolling Thunder, My Lai, body counts and body bags, the light at the end of the tunnel. Tet, Chicago, Kent State, the Pentagon Papers, "peace with honor," and impeachment without honor.

I was blessed.

I had a front-row seat as the big show rolled into town, because no one reflected and refracted the times like Ali did.

Watching him light the Olympic flame and hearing the astonished reaction of the eighty-five-thousand-plus crowd, I realized that a truly remarkable transformation had taken place.

A transformation in America and in him, or more specifically, in how those same Americans now viewed him.

No longer was he the outrageous, self-centered, badly behaved braggart who habitually humiliated his opponents—black and white. Gone was the reviled hypocrite who was manipulated by the Nation of Islam.

The unpatriotic draft dodger had been—thanks to the dearly paid-for realization that Vietnam was a deeply tragic disgrace—replaced by the prophet who spoke out when few did. And willingly paid the price.

"America—love it or leave it," the all-too-facile, hyperpatriotic slogan of the day declared.

In 1966, after his draft status was changed to 1-A and he made his instantly famous "I ain't got no quarrel with them Vietcong" remark, he was asked if he would (like other draft dodgers) leave the country. Something to consider with his money, connections, athletic ability, and fame.

But he wouldn't. Never even considered it.

"America is my birth country," he said. "They make the rules, and if they want to put me in jail, I'll go to jail. But I'm an American and I'm not running away."

"A foolish consistency is the hobgoblin of little minds," Ralph Waldo Emerson, my fellow New Englander, wrote some time ago.

But here was a consistency that was not so foolish. Indeed, it told us, I think, much about the champ politically.

Thirty-six years ago at that 1960 Rome Olympics, where he won the gold medal, he was approached right after the awards ceremony by a clearly anti-American Russian reporter looking for a juicy quote from the young boy. How did he feel, the reporter asked, about racial discrimination back home? This was the year, don't forget, of sit-ins and boycotts.

Cassius Clay didn't hesitate; he knew just what he felt: "Tell your readers we've got qualified people working on that problem, and I'm not worried about the outcome. To me the U.S.A. is still the best country in the world."

Last night, lighting the Olympic flame nearly four decades later, he was no longer Cassius Clay. Now he was Muhammad Ali, living legend.

And he had come full circle.

Atlanta Summer Olympics

On July 19, 1996, an estimated three billion people around the world watched as U.S. gold medal swimmer Janet Evans ran up the steep ramp of the stadium, holding the Olympic torch. She appeared to be the athlete chosen to light the Olympic flame.

Emerging from the shadows as a last-minute surprise was 1960 gold medal winner Muhammad Ali, who had been given the honor. The choice was a well-kept secret, and he is seen here watching the flame climb up to the Olympic torch.

★ 4 ★

ALI: IN HIS OWN WORDS

"You have to be a little crazy to be a fighter."

"When you want to talk about who made me, you talk to me. Who made me is me."

"And boxing made me feel like somebody different."

"I ain't no Superman. If the fans think I can do everything I say I can do, then they're crazier than I am."

"I know where I'm going and I know the truth,
and I don't have to be what you want me to be. I'm free to be what I want."

"Man, I ain't got no quarrel with them Vietcong."

"We're not all brothers; you can say we're brothers, but we're not."

"I would like to say to those of you who think I've lost so much, I have gained everything. I have peace of heart; I have a clear free conscience. And I'm proud. I wake up happy. I go to bed happy. And if I go to jail, I'll go to jail happy. Boys go to war and die for what they believe, so I don't see why the world is so shook up over me suffering for what I believe. What's so unusual about that?"

"America is my birth country. They make the rules, and if they want to put me in jail, I'll go to jail. But I'm an American and I'm not running away."

"Every day they die in Vietnam for nothing. I might as well die right here for something."

"I had to prove you could be a new kind of black man."

"I fought the best, because if you want to be a true champion,
you got to show people that you can whip everybody."

"We went to Manila as champions, Joe and me, and we came back as old men."

"It was the greatest fight of my life, and it wasn't about style, it was where I had to go for it, a place where you drop through a trapdoor."

"Now that I got my championship back every day is something special. I wake up in the morning, and no matter what the weather is like, every day is a sunny day."

ALI: IN HIS OWN TIME

1942

Cassius Marcellus Clay Jr. is born in Louisville, Kentucky (January 17).

President Franklin D. Roosevelt signs Executive Order 9066, forcing 100,000 Japanese Americans into internment camps.

Joe Louis, "The Brown Bomber," retains heavyweight crown.

1943

Rudolph Valentino Clay is born.

Race riot in Detroit, Michigan: 34 killed, 433 wounded.

Film *Stormy Weather*, starring Lena Horne, is released.

1944

D-day (June 6)

1945

Germany surrenders—VE-day (May 8).

U.S. drops atomic bombs on Hiroshima (August 6) and Nagasaki (August 9); Japan surrenders.

Ho Chi Minh forms provisional government in Vietnam.

Lt. Col. A. Peter Dewey becomes first U.S. soldier killed in Vietnam.

1946

President Harry S. Truman creates President's Commission on Civil Rights.

Benjamin Spock's *The Common Sense Book of Baby and Child Care* is published.

1947

Jackie Robinson becomes first black player in major league baseball.

1948

Harry S. Truman is reelected president.

1949

Vietnam state is established in Saigon.

George Orwell's *1984* is published.

Joe Louis retires.

1950

Korean War begins.

Ho Chi Minh declares Democratic Republic of Vietnam.

U.S. sends $15 million in military aid (money, men, and arms) to the French.

There are 1.5 million TV sets in American homes.

1951

J. D. Salinger's *The Catcher in the Rye* is published.

1952

Dwight D. Eisenhower is elected president.

There are 400 U.S. military advisers in Vietnam.

Doubleday & Company publishes English translation of Anne Frank's diary.

Alan Freed's Moondog Coronation Ball is staged in Cleveland.

1953

Ralph Ellison's *Invisible Man* wins National Book Award.

James Baldwin's *Go Tell It on the Mountain* is published.

Elvis Presley records "My Happiness" at the Memphis Recording Service.

1954

Cassius Clay begins boxing on local policeman's advice after bike gets stolen.

French defeated at Dien Bien Phu.

President Eisenhower explains his "domino theory" in historic press conference.

U.S. refuses to sign Geneva agreements regarding Vietnam.

In *Brown v. Board of Education* decision, Supreme Court rules segregation in public schools is unconstitutional.

William Golding's *Lord of the Flies* is published.

1955

U.S. sends aid to Saigon and begins training South Vietnamese soldiers.

Marian Anderson becomes first African American to sing with New York's Metropolitan Opera.

Fourteen-year-old Emmett Till is killed in Mississippi.

Rosa Parks refuses to give up her seat, precipitating the Montgomery, Alabama, bus boycott.

The emergence of Dr. Martin Luther King Jr.

Film *Blackboard Jungle* is released.

Disneyland opens.

Film *Rebel Without a Cause* is released.

1956

President Eisenhower is reelected.

French leave Vietnam.

Allen Ginsberg's *Howl and Other Poems* is published.

1957

Southern Christian Leadership Conference is founded.

President Eisenhower sends federal troops to enforce desegregation of schools in Little Rock, Arkansas.

Musical *West Side Story* premieres on Broadway.

1958

Cassius Clay meets Nation of Islam recruiter in Atlanta, Georgia.

Stereo recordings appear.

1959

Cassius Clay wins Golden Gloves and AAU tournaments.

Fidel Castro overthrows dictator and becomes premier of Cuba.

Berry Gordy founds Motown Records.

Publication and Broadway debut of Lorraine Hansberry's *A Raisin in the Sun*

1960

Cassius Clay graduates from Central High School, wins gold medal in light heavyweight boxing competition at Rome Olympics, and registers for draft.

Cassius Clay signs contract with Louisville Sponsoring Group, and wins first professional fight.

John F. Kennedy is elected president.

Sit-ins and boycotts take place in the South.

Student Non-Violent Coordinating Committee (SNCC) is formed.

Ruby Bridges becomes first black student to attend an all-white elementary school in the South.

Harper Lee's *To Kill a Mockingbird* is published.

1961

Cassius Clay hires Angelo Dundee as trainer.

Bay of Pigs invasion on Cuba

Freedom Riders take bus trips throughout the South to test enforcement of Supreme Court rulings outlawing segregated interstate travel; incidents occur in Anniston, Birmingham, and Montgomery, Alabama, and Jackson, Mississippi.

Albany Movement is formed in Georgia; Martin Luther King Jr. is arrested.

John Howard Griffin's *Black Like Me*, Joseph Heller's *Catch-22*, Robert Heinlein's *Stranger in a Strange Land*, and James Baldwin's *Nobody Knows My Name* are published.

1962

Cassius Clay defeats Archie Moore (KO, fourth round), hears Elijah Muhammad speak, and meets Malcolm X.

Cuban Missile Crisis

Number of military advisers in South Vietnam increases to 11,500.

James Meredith becomes first black student to register at University of Mississippi; Kennedy sends federal troops to stop rioting.

James Baldwin's *Another County*, Rachel Carson's *Silent Spring*, and Ken Kesey's *One Flew Over the Cuckoo's Nest* are published.

1963

Cassius Clay defeats Henry Cooper in the fifth round, appears on *Sports Illustrated* cover for first time.

President Kennedy is assassinated in Dallas, Texas (November 22).

Buddhists set themselves on fire to protest South Vietnamese government.

South Vietnam's premier Ngo Dinh Diem is murdered in U.S.-sanctioned coup.

Number of American military personnel in South Vietnam increases to 15,000.

Martin Luther King Jr. is arrested in Alabama, writes "Letter from Birmingham Jail."

Televised images of fire hoses and police dogs being used on African Americans, including children, in Birmingham shock nation.

Governor George Wallace refuses to allow two black students to enroll at University of Alabama.

Medgar Evers, NAACP field secretary, is murdered outside his home.

The March on Washington; King delivers "I Have a Dream" speech (August 28).

Four young girls are killed by bomb in Sixteenth Street Baptist Church in Birmingham, Alabama.

Bob Dylan's *The Freewheelin' Bob Dylan* is released.

Betty Friedan's *The Feminine Mystique* and Sylvia Plath's *The Bell Jar* are published.

1964

Cassius Clay defeats Sonny Liston (TKO, seventh round), becoming heavyweight champion (February 25), announces membership in Nation of Islam, announces name change to Muhammad Ali, marries Sonji Roi, and is reclassified 1-Y due to low scores on army intelligence tests.

Gulf of Tonkin Resolution passes, allowing war in Vietnam to begin.

Lyndon B. Johnson is elected president.

Twenty-Fourth Amendment abolishes poll tax.

Freedom Summer is launched to register black voters in Mississippi.

Three civil rights workers are killed by Ku Klux Klan in Mississippi.

Civil Rights Act is signed.

Martin Luther King Jr. is awarded Nobel Peace Prize.

Bob Dylan's *The Times They Are a-Changin'* is released.

1965

Muhammad Ali defeats Sonny Liston (KO, first round), retains title; defeats Floyd Patterson (KO, twelfth round), retains title.

Operation Rolling Thunder (the sustained aerial bombing of North Vietnam) begins.

First U.S. combat troops arrive in South Vietnam.

Battle of Ia Drang Valley

Number of U.S. soldiers in South Vietnam increases to 200,000.

Antiwar teach-in held at University of Michigan–Ann Arbor.

The Autobiography of Malcolm X is published.

Malcolm X is killed.

Bloody Sunday images—police using tear gas and clubs to attack marchers in Selma, Alabama—are shown on nightly news.

Voting Rights Act

Watts Riot: six days, thirty-four dead

Bill Cosby becomes first black actor to become a television star.

Bob Dylan plays amplified rock and roll at Newport Folk Festival.

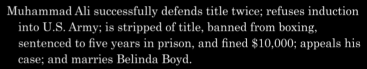

1966

Muhammad Ali divorces Sonji Roi, has draft status changed to 1-A, hires Herbert Muhammad as his manager, and successfully defends title six times, with five KOs.

Number of U.S. soldiers in South Vietnam increases to 300,000; 6,350 are killed in action (KIA).

James Meredith is shot during March Against Fear.

Stokely Carmichael uses term "black power."

Black Panther Party is formed.

John Sack's *M* is published.

1967

Muhammad Ali successfully defends title twice; refuses induction into U.S. Army; is stripped of title, banned from boxing, sentenced to five years in prison, and fined $10,000; appeals his case; and marries Belinda Boyd.

Number of U.S. soldiers in South Vietnam increases to 500,000; 11,363 KIA.

Martin Luther King Jr. speaks out against the war.

For the first time polls show most Americans oppose the war.

Thurgood Marshall becomes first African American appointed to Supreme Court.

Race riots in Newark, New Jersey, and Detroit, Michigan.

Beatles release *Sgt. Pepper's Lonely Hearts Club Band*.

Mary McCarthy's *Vietnam* and Jonathan Schell's *The Village of Ben Suc* are published.

Jonathan Kozol's *Death at an Early Age* is published.

Films *In the Heat of the Night* and *Guess Who's Coming to Dinner* are released.

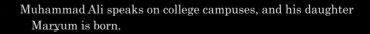

1968

Muhammad Ali speaks on college campuses, and his daughter Maryum is born.

North Vietnamese launch Tet Offensive.

My Lai massacre occurs.

Number of U.S. soldiers in South Vietnam reaches 543,000; 16,869 KIA.

Antiwar candidate Eugene McCarthy makes impressive showing in New Hampshire primary.

Robert Kennedy announces candidacy.

President Johnson announces he will not seek a second term.

Robert Kennedy is killed in Los Angeles.

Rioting at Democratic National Convention in Chicago.

Richard M. Nixon is elected president.

Martin Luther King Jr. is killed in Memphis, Tennessee.

Shirley Chisholm becomes first African American woman elected to Congress.

Mary McCarthy's *Hanoi* is published.

Tom Wolfe's *The Electric Kool-Aid Acid Test* is published.

1969

Troop withdrawals begin.

Number of U.S. soldiers in South Vietnam is 479,000; 11,780 KIA.

250,000 antiwar protesters in Washington, DC, as part of the Moratorium Against the Vietnam War

Life magazine publishes photographs of Americans killed in Vietnam in a single week.

500,000 attend outdoor concert near Woodstock, New York.

Beatles release *Abbey Road.*

Maya Angelou's *I Know Why the Caged Bird Sings* is published.

Charles Manson and others commit multiple murders.

1970

Muhammad Ali defeats Jerry Quarry (TKO, third round) and Oscar Bonavena (TKO, fifteenth round).

Joe Frazier becomes "official" heavyweight champion of the world.

Number of U.S. soldiers in South Vietnam is 280,000; 6,173 KIA.

President Nixon sends troops into Cambodia.

National Guardsmen kill four students at Kent State, in Ohio, during antiwar demonstrations.

1971

Muhammad Ali loses Fight of the Century to Joe Frazier in fifteen-round decision, has Supreme Court overturn conviction.

Number of U.S. soldiers in South Vietnam is 159,000; 2,414 KIA.

Lt. William Calley is convicted in My Lai trial.

Pentagon Papers are published.

1972

Muhammad Ali wins six fights.

Break-in at Watergate Hotel.

President Nixon is reelected.

Number of U.S. soldiers in South Vietnam is 24,000; 759 KIA.

Frances FitzGerald's *Fire in the Lake* and David Halberstam's *The Best and the Brightest* are published.

1973

Muhammad Ali loses to Ken Norton in twelve-round decision and wins three other fights, including return bout with Norton.

George Foreman defeats Joe Frazier, becoming heavyweight champion.

Draft ends; military is all volunteer.

Cease-fire agreement reached on Vietnam War; 68 KIA.

President Nixon announces "peace with honor."

1974

Muhammad Ali defeats Joe Frazier in twelve-round decision.

Ali defeats George Foreman in Rumble in the Jungle (KO, eighth round), reclaims title.

President Nixon resigns.

1975

Muhammad Ali defeats Joe Frazier in the Thrilla in Manila (fifteenth round), retains title; publishes autobiography, *The Greatest: My Own Story.*

Americans evacuate Saigon; war is over.

58,220 Americans killed in action

303,644 wounded in action

1,649 missing in action

250,000–500,000 Vietnamese civilians killed

1 million Vietnamese military killed in action

2 million Vietnamese wounded

Frank Robinson becomes first African American to manage MLB team.

1976

Muhammad Ali defeats Ken Norton in fifteen-round decision.

Ali divorces Belinda (now Khalilah) Ali.

Jimmy Carter is elected president.

U.S. issues Agent Orange report.

Black History Month is founded.

Alex Haley's *Roots: The Saga of an American Family* is published.

C. D. B. Bryan's *Friendly Fire* and Gloria Emerson's *Winners and Losers* are published.

Taxi Driver, directed by Martin Scorsese, is released.

One Flew Over the Cuckoo's Nest, directed by Milos Forman, wins five Oscars.

1977

Muhammad Ali successfully defends title twice.

Ali marries Veronica Porsche.

President Carter issues unconditional pardon to 10,000 draft evaders.

Andrew Young becomes first African American named as ambassador to United Nations.

Elvis Presley dies.

Philip Caputo's *A Rumor of War* is published.

Rocky, directed by John Avildsen, wins three Oscars, including Best Picture and Director.

1978

Muhammad Ali loses to Leon Spinks in fifteen-round decision.

Ali defeats Leon Spinks in fifteen-round decision, becomes first boxer to win heavyweight championship three times.

1979

Ali announces retirement.

Coming Home, directed by Hal Ashby, wins Oscars for Best Actor and Best Actress.

The Deer Hunter, directed by Michael Cimino, wins Oscars for Best Picture and Best Director.

1980

Muhammad Ali comes out of retirement and loses to Larry Holmes in tenth-round TKO.

U.S. helicopter commando mission to rescue hostages in Iran fails.

Ronald Reagan is elected president.

U.S. boycotts Moscow Olympics.

John Lennon is killed.

Apocalypse Now, directed by Francis Ford Coppola, wins Oscars for cinematography, sound.

1981

Muhammad Ali loses to Trevor Berbick in ten-round decision.

Ali retires.

Iranian hostages are released.

Sandra Day O'Connor becomes first woman named a Supreme Court justice.

1982

Vietnam Veterans Memorial is dedicated.

Michael Jackson releases *Thriller*, the top-selling album of all time.

1983

Alice Walker's *The Color Purple* is published, wins Pulitzer Prize.

1984

Muhammad Ali makes his Parkinson's syndrome public.

Ronald Reagan is elected president.

The Cosby Show first airs.

1985

Film *The Color Purple*, from Alice Walker's Pulitzer Prize–winning novel, is released.

1986

Muhammad Ali divorces Veronica Ali, marries Yolanda "Lonnie" Williams.

Martin Luther King Jr. Day is celebrated as national holiday.

1987

Muhammad Ali is named greatest heavyweight of all time by *The Ring* magazine.

Eyes on the Prize is shown on PBS.

1988
George H. W. Bush is elected president.

Toni Morrison's *Beloved* wins Pulitzer Prize.

1989
Colin Powell becomes first African American chairman of the Joint Chiefs of Staff.

Glory, directed by Edward Zwick, released.

1990
Muhammad Ali meets with Saddam Hussein, secures release of fourteen hostages.

Ali is inducted into International Boxing Hall of Fame.

1991
U.S. launches Operation Desert Storm against Iraq.

1992
Los Angeles race riots erupt.

Carol Moseley Braun becomes first African American woman elected to U.S. Senate.

Bill Clinton is elected president.

1993
A bomb explodes in the World Trade Center parking garage.

1994
North American Free Trade Agreement goes into effect.

1995
Million Man March in Washington, DC

1996
Bill Clinton is reelected president.

Muhammad Ali lights Olympic flame in Atlanta.

1997
Muhammad Ali given the Arthur Ashe Courage Award.

1998
Muhammad Ali is named United Nations Messenger of Peace.

1999
Muhammad Ali is named Sportsman of the Century by *Sports Illustrated*, appears on Wheaties box.

2000
George W. Bush is elected president.

2001
Muhammad Ali becomes spokesman for Coca-Cola.

Will Smith stars in movie of Ali's life.

September 11 terrorist attack on the World Trade Center occurs.

2002
Muhammad Ali's daughter Laila wins first boxing title.

2003
Saddam Hussein is captured.

2004
George W. Bush is reelected president.

2005
Muhammad Ali is awarded Presidential Medal of Freedom.

Muhammad Ali Center opens in Louisville, Kentucky.

2008
Barack Obama is elected first African American president.

2012
Muhammad Ali's seventieth birthday celebration

Barack Obama is reelected president.

Hurricane Sandy strikes.

2013
Boston Marathon terrorist attack occurs.

Nelson Mandela dies.

BIBLIOGRAPHY

4 Little Girls. Directed by Spike Lee. HBO Documentary Films, 1997. DVD.

Ali, Muhammad, with Hana Yasmeen Ali. *The Soul of a Butterfly: Reflections on Life's Journey*. New York: Simon & Schuster, 2004.

Ali, Muhammad, and Richard Durham. *The Greatest: My Own Story*. New York: Random House, 1975.

American Experience: Citizen King. Directed by Orlando Bagwell and W. Noland Walker. PBS Video, 2004. DVD.

American Experience: Freedom Riders. Directed by Stanley Nelson. PBS Video, 2011. DVD.

American Experience: Vietnam: A Television History. WGBH/PBS Video, 2004. DVD.

Bingham, Howard L., and Max Wallace. *Muhammad Ali's Greatest Fight: Cassius Clay vs. the United States of America*. Lanham, MD: M. Evans & Company, 2000.

Blum, John Morton. *Years of Discord: American Politics and Society, 1961–1974*. New York: W. W. Norton & Company, 1991.

Branch, Taylor. *At Canaan's Edge: America in the King Years 1965–68*. New York: Simon & Schuster, 2006.

———. *Parting the Waters: America in the King Years 1954–63*. New York: Simon & Schuster, 1988.

———. *Pillar of Fire: America in the King Years 1963–65*. New York: Simon & Schuster, 1998.

Brinkley, Douglas. *Rosa Parks: A Life*. New York: Penguin Books, 2000.

Cagin, Seth, and Philip Dray. *We Are Not Afraid: The Story of Goodman, Schwerner, and Chaney, and the Civil Rights Campaign for Mississippi*. New York: Macmillan, 1988.

Cosell, Howard. *Cosell*. New York: Playboy Press, 1973.

Cottrell, John. *Muhammad Ali, Who Once Was Cassius Clay*. New York: Funk & Wagnalls, 1967.

DeBenedetti, Charles. *An American Ordeal: The Antiwar Movement of the Vietnam Era*. Syracuse: Syracuse University Press, 1990.

Denenberg, Barry. *The True Story of J. Edgar Hoover and the FBI*. New York: Scholastic, 1993.

Duberman, Martin. *Howard Zinn: A Life on the Left*. New York: The New Press, 2012.

Dundee, Angelo, and Mike Winters. *I Only Talk Winning*. Chicago: Contemporary Books Inc., 1985.

Durant, John. *The Heavyweight Champions*. 5th ed. New York: Hastings House, 1973.

Early, Gerald. *The Culture of Bruising: Essays on Prizefighting, Literature, and Modern American Culture*. Hopewell, NJ: Ecco Press, 1994.

———. *The Muhammad Ali Reader*. New York: Rob Weisbach Books, 1998.

———. *Tuxedo Junction: Essays on American Culture*. Hopewell, NJ: Ecco Press, 1989.

Edmonds, Anthony O. *Muhammad Ali: A Biography*. Westport, CT: Greenwood Press, 2006.

Edwards, Harry. *The Revolt of the Black Athlete*. New York: Free Press, 1969.

Eyes on the Prize: America's Civil Rights Movement. Directed by Henry Hampton. Blackside Inc./PBS Video, 2006. DVD.

Ezra, Michael. *Muhammad Ali: The Making of an Icon*. Philadelphia: Temple University Press, 2009.

Foreman, George, and Joel Engel. *By George: The Autobiography of George Foreman*. New York: Villard Books, 1995.

Garrow, David J. *Bearing the Cross: Martin Luther King, Jr., and the Southern Christian Leadership Conference*. New York: Vintage Books, 1986.

Gitlin, Todd. *The Sixties: Years of Hope, Days of Rage*. New York: Bantam, 1989.

Goldman, Peter. *The Death and Life of Malcolm X*. Urbana: University of Illinois Press, 1979.

Hartmann, Douglas. *Race, Culture, and the Revolt of the Black Athlete: The 1968 Olympic Protests and Their Aftermath*. Chicago: University of Chicago Press, 2003.

Hauser, Thomas. *The Lost Legacy of Muhammad Ali*. Wilmington, DE: Sport Media Publishing, 2005.

———. *Muhammad Ali: His Life and Times*. London: Robson Books, 2004.

Huie, William Bradford. *Three Lives for Mississippi*. London: Heinemann, 1965.

Kram, Mark. *Ghosts of Manila: The Fateful Blood Feud Between Muhammad Ali and Joe Frazier*. New York: Harper, 2001.

Lewis, Claude. *Cassius Clay: A No-Holds-Barred Biography of Boxing's Most Controversial Champion*. New York: Macfadden-Bartell Corp., 1965.

Lipsyte, Robert. *Free to Be Muhammad Ali*. New York: Harper and Row, 1977.

———. *Sports World: An American Dreamland*. New York: Quadrangle/The New York Times Book Company, 1975.

Mailer, Norman. *The Fight*. New York: Vintage Books, 1975.

Marable, Manning. *Malcolm X: A Life of Reinvention*. New York: Viking, 2011.

Marqusee, Mike. *Redemption Song: Muhammad Ali and the Spirit of the Sixties*. London: Verso, 1999.

McWhorter, Diane. *Carry Me Home: Birmingham, Alabama: The Climatic Battle of the Civil Rights Revolution*. New York: Simon & Schuster, 2001.

Muhammad Ali: The Greatest, 1964–74. Directed by William Klein. Arte Video/Facets Video, 2002. DVD.

Nack, William. "Young Cassius Clay." *Sports Illustrated* (January 13, 1992): 70.

Oates, Joyce Carol. *On Boxing*. Expanded ed. New York: Ecco Books, 1987.

Olsen, Jack. *Black Is Best: The Riddle of Cassius Clay*. New York: Dell Publishing Co., 1967.

Olson, Lynne. *Freedom's Daughters: The Unsung Heroines of the Civil Rights Movement from 1830 to 1970*. New York: Touchstone, 2001.

O'Reilly, Kenneth. *"Racial Matters": The FBI's Secret File on Black America, 1960–1972*. New York: Free Press, 1989.

Parks, Rosa, and Jim Haskins. *Rosa Parks: My Story*. New York: Penguin Books, 1992.

Perry, Bruce. *Malcolm: The Life of the Man Who Changed Black America*. Barrytown, NY: Station Hill Press, Inc., 1991.

Remnick, David. *King of the World*. New York: Random House, 1998.

Sammons, Jeffrey T. *Beyond the Ring: The Role of Boxing in American Society*. Chicago: University of Illinois Press, 1990.

Shapiro, Fred R., ed. *The Yale Book of Quotations*. New Haven, CT: Yale University Press, 2006.

Sheed, Wilfrid. *Muhammad Ali: A Portrait in Words and Photographs*. New York: Thomas Y. Crowell, 1975.

Theoharis, Jeanne. *The Rebellious Life of Mrs. Rosa Parks*. Boston: Beacon, 2013.

Thrilla in Manila: Ali vs. Frazier. Directed by John Dower. Time Life Records, 2009. DVD.

Torres, José, and Bert Randolph Sugar. *Sting Like a Bee: The Muhammad Ali Story*. Chicago: Contemporary Books, 2002.

When We Were Kings. Directed by Leon Gast. PolyGram Filmed Entertainment/Gramercy Films, Universal Studios, 2002. DVD.

Williams, Juan. *Eyes on the Prize: America's Civil Rights Years 1954–1965*. New York: Penguin Books, 1987.

Zaroulis, Nancy and Gerald Sullivan. *Who Spoke Up?: American Protest Against the War in Vietnam 1963–1975*. Garden City, NY: Doubleday, 1984.